THE WINNING HABITS OF
STEVE JOBS

"An innovative view of personal empowerment seen through the lens of a technology pioneer's life."
— *Kirkus Review*

Dr. Robert M. Toguchi

STRATTON
—PRESS—
Publishing Life

THE WINNING HABITS OF STEVE JOBS
Copyright © 2020 **Dr. Robert M. Toguchi**

Stratton Press Publishing
831 N Tatnall Street Suite M #188,
Wilmington, DE 19801
www.stratton-press.com
1-888-323-7009

ISBN (Paperback): 978-1-64895-306-4
ISBN (Ebook): 978-1-64895-307-1

Printed in the United States of America

CONTENTS

PREFACE

*T*he *Winning Habits of Steve Jobs* was an outgrowth of a personal interest. Time has always been a priority in my life. In many ways, I began writing a book that I would most love to read with the interest of time in mind. *The Winning Habits of Steve Jobs* was designed to offer only the most pithy and insightful pieces of information that could potentially help any entrepreneur or rising professional to gain a competitive advantage in his or her career. In today's environment, young men and women do not have the luxury of time to get after the one or two key ideas that are most interesting to them. Communicators who write short articles, tweets, and concise radio messages recognize the value of their audience's time and delve into only those key facts that are relevant, pertinent, and compelling. In similar fashion, *The Winning Habits of Steve Jobs* strives to get after only those points that are essential to learn the most about Steve Jobs's initiatives and habits that led to his ultimate success.

Second, I have always been fascinated by truly remarkable individuals who have made a monumental difference in the course of history. The greater the impact of the individual, the more interesting they become. Quintessential figures such as Winston Churchill, Albert Einstein, Thomas

Edison, Martin Luther King Jr., Henry Ford, and others have always impressed me. Over time, I began to delve into the biographies of these remarkable persons so that I may gain an idea of what it took to make them so great. The intent of this book is to learn from another monumental figure of our time.

Third, I have recognized that habits play a critical role in the success of any individual. You can identify any key significant leader, and assuredly you can find selected key habits that led to their success. Distinct habits such as the deep desire of an inquisitive mind, dedicated excellence to achieving exceptional standards, motivational techniques of speech to move people, or getting individuals to feel special about what they are doing are all examples of how habits can make a difference in one's life. Often, we stumble through life, observing habits in a haphazard fashion without rhyme or reason, and only by chance do we find a mentor or friend to share their knowledge of a winning habit. *The Winning Habits of Steve Jobs* attempts to get out of the ad hoc manner in which we learn about habits and to refine this study of a field of knowledge that we'll get only after the very best habits of one of the most remarkable persons of all time.

Of note, a personal thanks to those who have helped with reviewing this work to include Tina Wamsley, Lee Chase, Robert Toguchi Jr., Rich Kirschke, Angela Forge, Victoria Principal, Barbara Misiaszek, and Dennis Montgomery, an Apple engineer. Additionally, none of this would have been possible without the favor of God.

INTRODUCTION

Habits are a part of everyone's life. They are inescapable. Habits form the basis of our personalities, they reflect our core values and beliefs, and they are unmistakable harbingers of future success. Often the product of early childhood experiences and personal observations, habits are generally ingrained in our personalities by the time we are nine years old.[1] Nonetheless, despite the early formation, every adult is capable of creating new habits and shedding old habits with a purposeful design. Recognition of this ability provides a unique opportunity for each individual to create his or her own path to great achievement. Success is within every person's reach. Steve Jobs was one of those talented entrepreneurs who conceived, developed, and refined winning habits that led to his tremendous success.

This book is more than a glimpse of those who are in the top 1 percent of the wealthiest persons in America. It is a look at a common, ordinary man who rose to the pinnacle of power through his personal means. This particular individual did not rely on a wealthy upbringing, was not a graduate of the Ivy League, and did not have a trust fund to rely upon as he made the journey into the halls of the rich and famous.

The Winning Habits of Steve Jobs provides insights for the average American household. How can a hardworking and motivated middle-income family person in America learn from others and get that break to make a difference? What does it take to make it to the top? Are there certain skills, habits, and behaviors that can be developed over time to increase the likelihood of any person's success? What breaks can the average hardworking individual count on to get through the difficulties and curveballs of life? These are just a few of the questions I address in *The Winning Habits of Steve Jobs.* This book focuses on one remarkable individual who relied upon his skills, habits, and behaviors to achieve success. Few could argue that Steve Jobs was not a man of great wealth. Listed in *Forbes* as one of the hundred richest men in America in 2012, Steve accumulated wealth topping $11 billion in assets. Even more than the dollar value, Steve created revolutionary products for the twenty-first century. He literally changed the behavior of people around the globe with the invention of the iPod, iMac, iPad, and iPhone. The social media revolution, which created billions in income for others, was a mere by-product of these iconic devices. Steve Jobs's creations changed the lives of Americans forever and spawned a tremendous consumer demand for these remarkable devices that few could have imagined in their lifetimes.

Early Background

One of America's most renowned and savvy billionaires, Steven Paul Jobs was not the product of a wealthy family. In fact, Steve Jobs was an orphan who was adopted into a family of modest means. Interestingly, Steve was not the only person of exceptional wealth to be offered up for adoption. This simple fact was not unusual when one considers the other notables of history who came from humble origins. Vidal Sassoon, Dave Thomas (the founder of Wendy's), Tom Monaghan (owner of Domino's Pizza), and L. L. Bean are just a few who were orphaned at an early age.

There was nothing exceptional about his biological parents. Steve Jobs's biological mother, Joanne Schieble, was a child of German heritage. She grew up in a rural town in the suburbs of Green Bay, Wisconsin, on a small farm. As a graduate student at the University of Wisconsin, Joanne Schieble dated and fell in love with Abdulfattah Jandali, a Muslim teacher from Syria. In the summer of 1954, Joanne traveled with Abdulfattah to Syria to meet his family. By the end of the summer, at the age of twenty-three, she discovered that she was pregnant. Joanne's strict Catholic father, Arthur Schieble, disapproved of the relationship—and threatened to disown her if she married Abdulfattah. An abortion was a difficult proposition for a young girl in a rural Catholic community. Hence, Joanne decided to travel to San Francisco in 1955 to work with the medical community to give her baby up for adoption.

Steve Jobs's adoptive family was not wealthy. Paul and Clara Jobs were a blue-collar Bay Area couple, neither of whom attended college. When Steve's biological mother discovered that the two lacked a college education, she refused to sign the adoption papers. With determination,

Schieble tried to relocate Steve to another family and only consented to the Jobs's adoption if they made a commitment to send him to college. Paul Jobs gained technical experience in several lines of work. Starting his career as a machinist in the US Coast Guard, Paul Jobs worked as a machinist in a company that manufactured lasers, served as a repossession man, demonstrated skills as a mechanic who restored cars, and later became a full-time used-car salesman. Clara Jobs was the daughter of an Armenian family that had fled the Turks to New Jersey and a responsible homemaker.

Steve Jobs was not brilliant. From all outside observers, he was not the best scientist, software developer, or engineer when it came to tinkering or innovation. Steve Wozniak, by far, was the true talent who was responsible for designing the original circuit boards and electronic part laydowns for the Apple I and II computers. Additionally, Jobs was not a great businessman. One of Steve's early advisers, Don Valentine, insisted that Steve receive external help from Mike Markkula since Jobs lacked even the most basic skills of writing a business plan for the fledgling business.

In summary, Steve Jobs was a disadvantaged youth from a middle-class family. He essentially lacked business experience, financial capital, and technical smarts. Neither of his parents had a college education. From this viewpoint, the normal characteristics of a successful entrepreneur were scarcely evident. To what can we attribute the remarkable and phenomenal success of one of America's top billionaire entrepreneurs—and arguably the most innovative technology leader of the early twenty-first century? This discussion will emphasize the role that simple habits of success, developed over time, played in forging and developing the Steve Jobs who became an unqualified success to a generation of Americans who recognize him as the founder of Apple Inc.

CHAPTER 1

Winning Habits

Habits are all around us. People routinely do things every day without even thinking about them. Whether starting a car, booting up a laptop, making a cup of coffee in the morning, parallel parking, or going through a daily exercise routine, the pattern of one's behavior is generally firmly ingrained in the subconscious mind and done flawlessly without even thinking about them.

Researchers note that successful habits are the foundation for success at work. Those who establish successful habits are more likely to succeed on the job, on the project, in the boardroom, or on the athletic field. Time and time again, professional coaches have emphasized and explained that the critical key to success in any walk of life is establishing and maintaining successful performance habits.

Entire books have been written about how to form habits and how to break them. Charles Duhigg's *The Power of Habit* (2012) explores the subject of why we do what we do and how entire businesses are now looking at the basics of habit formations to improve how they market products and sell them in the marketplace. Businesses such as Starbucks are discovering that successful employee habits help create opportunities and make the sales that are essential to the bottom line.

Steve Jobs created and tailored his habits to achieve his goals. He realized that habits were the venue to get after his goals. He recognized that habits can fundamentally change your life relatively quickly on a semipermanent basis; over time, they can literally change your life forever. With the right habits, a person can create and achieve personal success. Steve was able, over time, to create his own habits and recreate himself to achieve success. With the right habits for success, Steve Jobs's potential became limitless.

What Is a Habit?

What exactly is a *habit?* A habit can be defined as "an acquired mode of behavior that has become nearly or completely involuntary."[2] Another definition of habit can be "a behavior pattern acquired by frequent repetition of physiologic exposure that shows itself in regularity or increased facility of performance."[3] As such, habits are behaviors that individuals acquire over time and generally occur during the course of one's formative years of learning. Steve Jobs was no exception, and he developed these unique habits over a period of years.

Recent research has revealed that habits emerge because the human brain is constantly seeking ways to reduce effort.[4] Without interference, the brain will attempt to make almost all routine actions a habit since it allows the brain to conserve energy and become more efficient.

Research indicates that greater efficiency in brain activities has proven to reduce the size of the brain.[5] Efficiency also allows the brain to focus on more important tasks that require concentration and power, such as learning new skills, navigating through difficulties, and executing projects with great complexity. Creating habits streamlines activities for the brain and allows the brain to focus on what is important.

Habits Are Valuable

To many competitors, habits are critical and essential for success. World-class performers such as Michael Phelps rely on habits to achieve greatness. As an Olympic athlete and world-record breaker, Michael Phelps developed a training regimen that maximized the development of habits so that his execution and reactions under stress would become instinctive.

Habits prepare entrepreneurs for the storm. Every business will face crises that require uncompromising faith and commitment. What prepares the entrepreneurs for the crises that come unexpectedly when everything seems to be going well? Habits provide entrepreneurs with resiliency, relevant steps, and best practices that steer the business in the midst of insurmountable odds. Resiliency can come in the form of financial reserves, reliable partners, network relationships, and uncommon investors who can intervene for the business in times of crisis. By being prepared, periods of crisis can be dealt with in a much calmer fashion since strategic hedges and practical steps to address the crisis have been thought about in advance. In short, appropriate habits help entrepreneurs weather the storms of life.

Habits also prepare entrepreneurs for the doldrums. Habits can serve to carry a leader through challenging times where nothing seems to be improving. Businesses can hit plateaus when profits are flat or in steady decline. Habits serve as the necessary bridge to better times since they provide leadership behaviors that are tried and true. When an entrepreneur feels that he or she is in decline, each can rely on the steadfastness of proven habits and proven values to bring the business or the enterprise back on track. Winning habits pave the way for individuals to restore entrepreneurial success through proven best practices to reestablish the foundation and right the ship.

Habits prepare entrepreneurs for the next level of excellence. Excellence in business requires time to invest in researching the product, knowing the business climate, finding the right partners, supervising the workforce, and making the right investments. Time is indispensable. The beauty of successful habits is that they free the mind to focus on time investments that truly matter. Successful habits unclutter your business day by making routine the daily decisions that are essential for smooth and error-free operations. Supplier order decisions, payroll management, marketing practices, and production line execution can all be routinized through the acceptance of successful habits. Habits free up your operational time, which is essential to business success.

Steve Jobs knew that he had developed winning habits. He trusted his thought patterns, his instincts, and his habits to bring him through the difficult years after being fired from Apple. Winning habits gave him the critical first steps that enabled him to rapidly start new ventures in NeXT and Pixar. It also gave him the foundational values, skills, and attributes necessary to bring about the turnaround at Apple when the board of advisers brought him back as the interim CEO. In all of this, winning habits were the essential ingredients that made Jobs a successful CEO in the early twenty-first century. These habits made him a world-class leader for challenging times.

How Are Habits Formed?

Habits are formed through recognizable patterns. In *The Power of Habit*, Charles Duhigg notes that every habit begins with a pattern called a pattern loop. First, there is a trigger or a cue that signals your brain to transfer to automatic mode. This initiates a second step or a routine that is already wired in your brain. The third step is the reward. This reward is the necessary ingredient to reinforce the decision to execute the habit. It lets the brain know that there is a real benefit from doing the habit; this improved-behavior routine results in a feeling of satisfaction.

Habits are formed in the brain. A part of the brain called the basal ganglia is known to govern the practice of habits. About the size of a golf ball, the basal ganglion is located deep within the central section of the brain beneath the cerebral cortex. The basal ganglia is the unconscious control center for habits. It decides when to activate a habit, and it tells the brain when to turn on specific brain cells. Once activated, we automatically start a thought process, a specific routine behavior, or a decision-making process.

The neuron or brain cell is the core component of the brain. A neuron is an electrically excitable cell that processes and transmits information by electrochemical signaling.

The average brain has about one hundred trillion neurons. Each neuron can be connected to up to ten thousand other neurons, thereby passing signals to each other using as many as a quadrillion synapses or connections. It is through these synapses that habits are created and then reinforced through practice.

Habits Affect Brain Cells

It is apparent that habits are created over long periods of repetitive thinking and repetitious behavior. As a result, habits are also the outcome or by-product of certain brain cells repeatedly communicating with one another. The brain cell communications or electronic chatter is called a synapse. The more frequently that a brain cell converses with another brain cell, the synapse becomes stronger and stronger. Those brain cells that communicate regularly are, to some degree, married to each other. Oftentimes, these two brain cells are connected with each other for life. Due to this repetition, the basal ganglia mentioned above labels these connections as *habits*. After the basal ganglia labels the brain cells as habits, those designated brain cells remain habits forever. They rarely ever get unstuck. In most cases, these habits are labeled forever. The basal ganglia will keep it that way—unless you learn how to train your brain to get rid of those habits.

How Are Habits Changed?

Habits are not always easy to change. Depending on the longevity of the habit, the ability to overcome or to change a habit can be a difficult experience. Nonetheless, while habits are difficult to change, the process is possible. There are several known ways to accomplish habit change, and they include making to-do lists of new habits, providing inhibitors of bad habits, and combining or merging new habits with old habits.

Make To-Do Lists

Making a to-do list of new habits is a way to schedule your new habit.[6] The vast majority of persons of wealth maintain to-do lists. Since the to-do list is a personal management tool for time and tasks, adding a new habit is a routine way to ensure that the new tasks are scheduled into the day. If they are simple habits, such as taking thirty minutes to schedule your day or adding a glass of water to your morning routine, they will become new additions with relative ease. After several weeks, simple habits will become a routine part of your daily activities.

Create Inhibitors of Bad Habits

Bad habits are undesirable. In order to move toward the creation of good habits, it is important to slowly cease bad habits to make room for self-improvement. One simple technique for reducing bad habits is to provide inhibitors for bad habits. For example, if excessive smoking at your workplace is a bad habit, consider leaving your lighter in your car and reduce the number of cigarettes that you have on hand. By creating an inconvenience of access to your lighter or having to go to the local store for more, you make it difficult to sustain your bad habit of smoking an excessive number of cigarettes. Over time, bad habits can be minimized or completely eliminated due to inhibitors.

Habit Stacking—Combine Old Habits with New Habits

It is much easier to add a new habit by combining it with an old habit than to create a competition between a new habit and an old habit. View the old habit as a routine that occurs in a groove. It is easier to create a new habit in a parallel groove than to turn it in an opposing direction. The brain is already programmed to execute the old habit, but by adding a new habit to the old routine, the brain is more accepting of the new routine.

If your new habit is to eat a piece of fruit every morning, it is easier to combine the fruit in the same bowl of cereal each day. If the new habit is to drink a glass of water each morning, consider adding this to the old routine of drinking a cup of coffee. Combining these habits would be to drink a cup of coffee followed by a glass of water. This technique is also characterized as *habit stacking*[7] since new habits are layered over the older habits. Of paramount importance is knowing which habits are essential for entrepreneurial success. In this regard, studying the winning habits of Steve Jobs and inculcating them into your personal lifestyle are investments with real benefits.

Where Do We Learn New Habits?

In general, habits come from people they are most closely associated with. In most cases, the most influential people in a person's life are his or her parents. A young person adopts the vast majority of his or her habits in early childhood. According to a recent study at Brown University, Dr. Rebecca Jackson claims that habits in children are unlikely to be altered after age nine.[8] With these study results, it is apparent that parents play an important role in mentoring their children. With the right parental role model, several millionaires have revealed that at least one parent of wealth had been influential in teaching them habits of success.[9]

Habits are also generated by observing people around us. Our associates in early childhood, educational experiences, business associates, and friends are sources of new habits. Studies indicate that we learn habits from neighborhood parental figures, elementary and secondary school teachers, college professors, supervisors, informal education, formal education, work experiences, and American culture. Millionaire author Robert Kiyosaki noted in his best-selling *Rich Dad, Poor Dad* that his observations of his two fathers, one rich and one poor, taught him the successful habits that differentiate the poor from those who attain great wealth.[10] Knowing that habits come from observed behavior, we can create associations with people who can contribute to the development of new habits. Successful people have relied upon mentors. Those who have attributed their success to their mentors include Bill Gates (Warren Buffett), Oprah Winfrey (Maya Angelou),

Yves Saint Laurent (Christian Dior), Richard Branson (Sir Francis Laker), and Mark Zuckerberg (Steve Jobs).[11] The relationship between mentors and successful entrepreneurs is well-established, and many realize the value of these personal connections in accelerating growth and maturity in a young professional.

New successful habits can be learned from observing the behaviors of other successful leaders. One particular individual who controlled his environment, his associations, his mentors, and his personal habits was Steve Jobs. Steve invested deeply into shaping his environment, his experiences, his associates, and his time. If anyone could provide the ultimate example of what it takes to observe, emulate, acquire, and sustain successful habits, it was Steve Jobs.

The Daily Habits of Steve Jobs

> When I was seventeen, I read a quote that went something like: "If you live each day as if it was your last, someday you'll most certainly be right." It made an impression on me, and since then, for the past thirty-three years, I have looked in the mirror every morning and asked myself: "If today were the last day of my life, would I want to do what I am about to do today?" And whenever the answer has been no for too many days in a row, I know I need to change something.
>
> —Steve Jobs

Wealthy entrepreneur Benjamin Franklin stated, "Your net worth to the world is usually determined by what remains after your bad habits are subtracted from your good ones." The decision to plan your time is purposeful and active.

Create an effective daily routine that leads toward the establishment of an abundance of good habits.

There are at least three direct benefits from a well-planned daily routine. First, a daily routine provides structure and familiarity. This structure can provide you with a sense of organization and ownership of your life. Second, a daily routine can lead toward activities that generate personal happiness, peace of mind, and satisfaction through the achievement of overall simplicity. Last, a planned daily routine streamlines effort and generally increases the overall efficiency in your life.

A snapshot of the daily habits of Steve Jobs provides an insight into what he valued and believed in. Steve valued interacting on a personal level with his close team, focusing his time on his highest priorities at work, and spending time with his family. Emotional interaction, focus, and family commitment were clearly important values for him. Instead of allowing distractions to affect his life, Steve took control of his time through closely monitored habits. Values drove his habits, and habits drove his daily routine.

Steve Jobs was an early riser. Reflecting his passion to excel at Apple, he typically started his day at six o'clock[12] to get after his agenda with personal drive and spirit. He entered his day with great excitement and a passion to make a difference in his companies. At one point, he was CEO of Pixar and CEO at Apple. He quickly learned how to del-

egate to top-notch professionals at Apple with the likes of
Jonathan Ive as the head of the designs group, Avi Tevanian
running software, Jon Rubinstein in charge of engineering,
and Tim Cook as head of manufacturing. To get after his
vision, Steve learned how to acquire and keep the best talents in the industry.

His morning routine was highly productive. Steve
relied on his habit of holding face-to-face meetings in the
mornings with Apple's product and management teams.[13]
He relished the opportunity for personal contact and to
hold an exchange to focus on the future products being
developed by his designers. He observed that the digital age could take you away from face-to-face encounters
with the penchant for Skype, e-mail, or texting. However,
there was true value to be gained from hashing things out
face-to-face with emotion, yelling, hugging, and scream-
ing. The personal encounters with his team members were
an important part of his daily routine. Steve clearly valued personal face-to-face dynamics with people to high-
light the importance of the personal touch in business
and achieving overall success.

In the afternoons, Steve would commit to meeting
with Jony Ive at the Apple Design Center on the first floor
of their building in Cupertino, California. The environment for the design center was extremely well-controlled
with views of beautiful landscaped trees, frost-tinted
windows, and soothing background music in the genre
of jazz or new age tones. The floor layout would be spa-
cious with eight elongated tables and scores of models of
future product designs for Apple. Rather than listening to
a PowerPoint brief, Steve wanted to feel the texture and

quality of his products and discuss detailed improvements to their design. He focused on the product. His habit was to embrace the hands-on experience. Steve Jobs valued the impression that the actual product would have on the consumer. While others may spend time with the manufacturing processes, the supply inventory, or the building design, Steve placed his greatest emphasis on the actual product. It was the product focus that would represent the brand and star quality for Apple and Steve Jobs.

In the evenings, Steve preferred to spend time with his immediate family. He shied away from life as a celebrity. Rather than embracing gala events, formal dinners, celebrations, or festivities, Steve enjoyed the simplicity of a family meal, nestled around a long wooden table with his wife and children. He was consistent in his daily habit of spending time with his close family every night at dinner. Steve valued his family relationships and the closeness of his children, and he put them ahead of celebrities and entertainment.

Of great significance to his success was Steve Jobs's daily habit of ruthless focus. Focus was all about making every minute count toward the tasks that were truly important to his success. Steve learned how to separate the wheat from the chaff. His staff would daily inundate Steve with routine issues of personnel actions, legal problems, or administrative tasks. Steve would just give them a blank stare or a blank response in an e-mail. Instead of dealing with mundane problems, Steve would "pick out four or five things that were really important for him to focus on and then just filter out—almost brutally—filter out the rest." That's what highly successful leaders do—they manage their time and focus on what is vitally important to their success.

From the survey of his daily habits, it is evident that he "connected the dots" in his lifestyle. Unlike others, there was no randomness to his daily habits. There was no presence of an ad hoc approach to his daily routines and routine decisions. Clearly, Steve knew what he hoped to achieve during his lifetime and aligned his values with his goals and his daily habits to support that vision. Controlling his environment, his associations, his mentors, and his time were important factors that led to Steve's success as an entrepreneur.

His daily habits reflected his core values. Steve Jobs clearly valued spending time with his close family, his personal interaction with people, his quest to develop the best possible products for society, and his desire to make Apple a preeminent company and an integral part of his lifelong legacy. A close review of his daily habits reveals a purposeful alignment between his values, his goals, and his habits. An end-to-end approach to design was applied to Steve's own lifestyle.

John C. Maxwell, the author of *The Daily Routine of Successful Leaders*, said, "The first step in determining your daily routine is figuring out what really matters to you. You can't prioritize if you don't know your priorities."[14] There are kernels of wisdom in what John Maxwell is conveying. The remarkable feature of Steve Jobs's daily habits was that he configured these habits to reflect his priorities, his goals, and his dreams. He went beyond merely accepting the normal best habits; he tailored them to match his vision of where he was going. In all things, daily habits are a great harbinger of what you will become.

A Framework for Exploring Steve Jobs's Winning Habits: Character, Knowledge, and Execution

Habits come in all forms and variations. There is no shortage of ways in which habits can manifest themselves. For starters, we find habits in throwing a baseball, swinging a baseball bat, running the bases, sliding in at home plate, and virtually any specific routine found in sports. Habits can be found at the office—whether it is making the office rounds, writing a to-do checklist, initiating a meeting, setting up a business luncheon, or brainstorming the next major project for the company. Habits can be prevalent even in our thoughts. Whether it is questioning or posing problems, listening and understanding, generating alternatives, setting company standards, or thinking interdependently—all of these approaches are products of human habit. In essence, these are all products of learned behavior over time.

To help frame our thinking about Steve Jobs's winning habits, we will explore the basic categories of character, knowledge, and execution. Character can be described as all the related habits, behaviors, and activities that formed the essential traits and attributes of Jobs during his early years. Knowledge can be attributed to those skill sets, understanding of context, and basic understanding of the facts that Jobs would need to be thoroughly proficient in his line of work and to excel as a business entrepreneur in a field full of competition.

Execution is related to those habits of remarkable execution that all great firms need to keep the train on its track and deliver superior products, goods, and services at or above the industry standard.

CHAPTER 2

Winning Habits of Character

*M*erriam-Webster defines *character* as a "complex of mental and ethical traits" that are distinctive to an individual. It implies that the character qualities and character traits help determine how a person will respond in any given situation. In many cases, success or failure in a particular situation may depend on how an individual responds to given circumstances or situations. Sound character is often a determinant of success. This chapter will delve into the unique character habits of Steve Jobs that contributed to his success as an entrepreneur.

Habit of Character: An Inquisitive Mind

What exactly is an inquisitive mind? A person with an inquisitive mind could be considered someone who is given to inquiry, research, and knowing more about a particular subject area. He or she is generally disposed to asking hard questions and seems eager to gain knowledge. Those with inquisitive minds are intellectually curious and tend to delve into a layer of detail that is beyond normal expectations. Of note, many of the individuals below fell into the category of entrepreneurs who possessed inquisitive minds.

Steve Jobs held an ingrained habit of voracious curiosity. He did not direct his curiosity to only those things that would make himself successful; he was naturally inquisitive. As an example, early in his career, Jobs held a deep desire to learn about calligraphy and delve into all the intricate variations that were possible. His inquisitive habit paid off. Later, the wide selection of calligraphy symbols would become one of the features that made the original Apple computer so successful.[15]

Jeff Bezos, the founder of Amazon, possesses an inquisitive mind. With a net worth of more than $200 billion, Bezos learns constantly from the current trends in business and is willing to take a hard turn toward winning ideas. Prior to becoming an entrepreneur in 1994, Bezos served as a senior vice president at D. E. Shaw and Company, a wealthy hedge fund. A constant learner, Bezos discovered that the World Wide Web was growing at a phenomenal rate of "2,300 percent a month."[16] Seeing an opportunity, he developed a list of more than twenty products that could be sold over the Internet through online sales. He selected books, and the rest became Amazon history. Amazon today is a multibillion-dollar company and continues to expand into other types of online product sales at a remarkable rate.

Elon Musk, the founder of SpaceX, Tesla Motors, and X.com, is a true believer in self-learning. With a remarkable appetite for reading, he is known to have read the entire *Encyclopedia Britannica*, and he completed a six-month BASIC programming course in three days.[17] When he was in grade school, he was reported to have consistently devoted ten hours a day to reading. This inquisitive nature extended to his commercial prospects. At the age of twelve, he used his BASIC programming skills to write the program Blastar, a video game he sold to *PC and Office Technology* for a small profit. This basic inquisitive habit extended to prospects in space exploration, designer cars, PayPal software, and a variety of unique interests.

Bill Gates, the founder of Microsoft, is known to have a highly inquisitive mind. With a reported net worth of more than $115 billion, Bill Gates is characterized as a voracious reader. During an interview with Bill Gates's father, the elderly gentleman claimed that "just about every kind of book interests him…encyclopedias, science fiction, you name it."[18] He was such a bookworm as a young boy that the family had to establish rules against reading at the dinner table. Bill Gates continues his habit of exploratory reading. His personal blog, GatesNotes, features more than 150 books for recommended reading, ranging from histories of science to novels.[19]

Warren Buffett, the owner of Berkshire Hathaway, has taken over companies such as IBM and H. J. Heinz. He is well-known as a reader with an inquisitive mind. At the age of eighty-eight—and with reported net worth of more than $81 billion—Warren Buffett attributes much of his success to learning. When asked about the key to his success, he pointed to a large stack of books and said, "Read five hundred pages of this every day. That's how knowledge works.

It builds up like compound interest. All of you can do it, but I guarantee not many of you will do it."[20]

Larry Ellison, the founder of Oracle Corporation, claims that his inquisitive nature is largely responsible for his success. During an interview, he stated, "The most important aspect of my personality, as far as determining my success goes, has been my questioning conventional wisdom, doubting experts, and questioning authority."[21] Additionally, he noted, "While that can be very painful in your relationships with your parents and teachers, it's enormously useful in life." The inquisitive mind proved valuable over his career. Interestingly, Larry Ellison started Oracle with an investment of only $1,200.[22]

The habit of an inquisitive mind has been a common characteristic of many of the most successful individuals. The spark of interest and intellectual curiosity has inspired some of the greatest entrepreneurial minds in America. Jeff Bezos, Elon Musk, Bill Gates, Warren Buffett, Larry Ellison, and Steve Jobs fostered this exceptional habit. You, too, can embrace this habit. Repeated investments in reading or other forms of intellectual curiosity can lead to a desire to learn each day. Making intellectual curiosity a part of one's daily routine can pay big dividends during the course of a career.

Habit of Character: Guard Your Heart and Follow Your Passion

> Your work is going to fill a large part
> of your life, and the only way to be
> truly satisfied is to do what you believe

is great work. And the only way to do great work is to love what you do. If you haven't found it yet, keep looking. Don't settle. As with all matters of the heart, you'll know when you find it.

—Steve Jobs

Unless you have a lot of passion about this, you're not going to survive.

—Steve Jobs

Steve Jobs embraced the daily habit of following his passion. For Jobs, it wasn't about the money. He knew how to focus his efforts to follow what was near and dear to his heart. He realized that passion would enable him to invest the necessary time and energy to become a success in the career field of his choice. Passion would carry him through the difficult times and inspire him to continue the journey when all others had given up. Passion was the necessary and critical habit to build his bridge to career success.

Steve Jobs had to choose between following his passion or making money. In several cases, Jobs lost money doing what he believed was the right thing to do. His return to Apple after being fired and spending years with NeXT and Pixar was less about making money than about doing what he knew was the right thing.

After being let go from Apple in 1985, Steve Jobs pursued his passion in computers and searched for the next big breakthrough. Biochemistry was an emerging field with great potential. In August, Stanford biochemist Paul

Berg met with Steve to discuss the significant advances being made in recombinant DNA, molecular cloning, and gene splicing. While highlighting the difficulties in the process, Berg explained how computers lacked the ability to simulate these biological experiments in the lab since the computers that could handle such capacities were just too expensive.[23] This problem stimulated Jobs's thinking and made him excited and passionate about exploring the possibilities of an academically focused computer with the power to serve the needs of a university lab.

The new project of designing a computer for the high-end academic market fit nicely with Steve's passion. In 1983, Steve had visited the computer science department at Brown University in Rhode Island. He was very interested in listening to the needs of academic professors. These researchers expressed a common interest: the desire to have a workstation that combined both characteristics of being "powerful and personal."[24] Jobs had a personal interest in this proposition. While serving as the head of the Macintosh Division, Steve initiated a project to create such a workstation. It was dubbed the Big Mac. The plan was to have a powerful Unix operating system coupled with the user-friendly GUI interface of Macintosh. After Steve left his job at Apple, the new chief, Jean-Louis Gassee, killed the project. Jobs did not give up.

Fellow workers at Apple shared Steve Jobs's passion for a new operating system that could solve the problem. Rich Page, the key engineer for the Big Mac's chip design, wanted to continue the Big Mac initiative. Bud Tribble, a software design engineer for the Macintosh, expressed a similar interest in starting a new company to pursue the idea of a workstation with power and a personal touch. Bud also managed to gain the support of two other Macintosh division employees. George Crow was an engineer, and Susan Barnes was a controller. A fifth person—marketing specialist Daniel Lewin—was wooed by Jobs and came over to the breakaway team because he believed in the possibilities of a new company with Jobs at the helm. With passion and excitement, Steve was able to pursue his dream and convince five others to make the break with him.

> Have the courage to follow your heart and intuition. They somehow know what you truly want to become.
> —Steve Jobs

Passion for Pursuit at Pixar

A similar passion for a new breakthrough idea sparked Steve Jobs's interest with Pixar. When Jobs was losing his support at Apple in the summer of 1985, he met with Alan Kay, the former Xerox PARC employee and then a current fellow with Apple. Realizing Steve's interest in the connectivity between technology and creative art, Alan Kay arranged a meeting with his friend Ed Catmull, leader of the computer division in George Lucas's film studio. What Jobs observed at the studio blew him away.

The artistic creation of powerful digital images was the focus of George Lucas's computer division. This unit built and blended the hardware and software components of this highly complex activity. Within this division, John Lasseter led a small group of extremely creative people who were

DR. ROBERT M. TOGUCHI

making short computer animation videos for the commercial market. Their talent would become increasingly apparent as the team matured.

At the same time, George Lucas was experiencing personal challenges. After completing the first *Star Wars* trilogy, George was undergoing a contentious divorce with his spouse and needed to raise funds quickly. He decided to sell the computer division. Ed Catmull was notified to expedite the sale and was relieved at the timely arrival of Steve Jobs.

Steve Jobs loved computer graphics. He knew where he had deep passion, and the computer division gave him the opportunity to become immersed with the possibilities of computer animation. To follow his passion, Steve offered George Lucas $5 million to take over the division—and another $5 million to finance the establishment of the division as a stand-alone company. The timing was right. Even though George Lucas wanted a lot more, he agreed to sell the division. Steve owned 70 percent of the company, and the rest was given to the forty founding employees of the firm. The division was originally called the Graphics Group, and later changed its name to Pixar Animation Studios.

The computer animation part of Pixar became quite successful. Unlike its faltering hardware counterpart, the computer animation short entitled "Luxo Jr." became a hit in 1986 at SIGGRAPH, the largest convention for the computer graphics industry. Pixar caught the attention of Walt Disney executives, which brought about small projects and a relationship with America's top animation producer for the film industry. The successful relationship with Walt

Disney Feature Animation grew to a point where Disney signed a deal for $26 million to produce three computer-animated films. The first of the films was *Toy Story*, and the rest is history. *Toy Story*'s box office success led to gross sales of more than $362 million worldwide. Jobs's passion for computer animation had paid off. Pixar would go on to create other blockbuster movies, including *A Bug's Life*, *Toy Story 2*, *The Incredibles*, *Cars*, *Ratatouille*, *Toy Story 3*, *Frozen*, *Brave*, and *Finding Dory*. Few companies can boast of the tremendous success of Pixar, and all of it was driven by the passion of Jobs and the amazing creative talent of Ed Catmull, Andrew Stanton, Pete Docter, Lee Unkrich, Brad Bird, and John Lasseter. In the end, passion can lead to considerable benefits.

Passion is an important step toward remarkable success. Those who embrace their passions and choose career paths that inspire these passions find work in their chosen professions to be a pleasure. Steve Jobs chose to embrace his passion. Instead of pursuing projects for purely monetary benefit, Steve prioritized his time to do only those things that brought him personal satisfaction. You, too, can foster this habit. Recognize the career profession that brings you happiness. Seek professional development experiences, education, and mentors that can move you toward your ideal profession. By not settling for second best, Jobs was able to convert what he enjoyed most and found tremendous career success.

Habit of Character: Be a Committed Problem Solver

> Being the richest man in the cemetery
> doesn't matter to me...going to bed
> at night saying we've done something
> wonderful...that's what matters to me.
> —Steve Jobs

> When you first start off trying to solve
> a problem, the first solutions you come
> up with are very complex, and most
> people stop there. But if you keep going,
> and live with the problem and peel
> more layers of the onion off, you can
> oftentimes arrive at some very elegant
> and simple solutions. Most people just
> don't put in the time or energy to get
> there. We believe that customers are
> smart, and want objects which are well
> thought through.
> —Steve Jobs

Problem solving is a characteristic feature of most wealthy individuals. Whether it is Elon Musk, Jeff Bezos, Mark Zuckerberg, or Bill Gates, every individual who has accumulated great wealth has refined the habits of the inquisitive mind and problem solving. Wealthy entrepreneurs are not satisfied with the status quo. In every aspect of their lives, they are constantly exploring the ways that things could be improved and how the lives of many in the world can be touched by solving problems. By solving a problem that billions confront every day, great men and women attain billionaire status. Solve a problem that a few people need solved can make you a small profit. Solve a problem that millions need solved—and you literally become a billionaire. The math is actually quite simple.

Billionaires solve big problems. Steve Jobs was not alone on taking on big problems. Bill Gates believed that he needed to invest in big problems that governments around the world were incapable of solving.[25] His foundation works on finding a cure for malaria. Jeff Bezos recognized that the Internet was growing at a pace of 2,400 percent annually.[26] He matched the problem of linking book distributors to the Internet on a massive scale and launched Amazon.com, which turned into a billion-dollar company.

Mark Zuckerberg was introduced to a social networking site called The Harvard Connection, which allowed members to post their photographs, personal links, and personal information to close associates and friends within the Harvard community. Discontent with the limitations of a small university community, Mark solved the software problems that enabled a much wider distribution of network services to universities across the country. With the help of outside investors such as Peter Thiel, founder of PayPal, Zuckerberg's social network site grew to more than a million users in one year.[27] The rest is history. Each innovator recognized the problem, seized the initiative, and developed solutions that provided handsome rewards.

From his earliest days, Steve Jobs nurtured the habit of solving problems. It was unique to his character. Jobs wondered how a product could be created or how to improve an existing product. He had a clairvoyant way of looking at a device and identifying the numerous ways that it could work better, and he could pinpoint the problems that needed to be solved.

Steve Jobs's work in the development of the iPhone reflects his habit of problem solving. In 2005, iPod sales were taking off exponentially with annual sales of more than $20 million. The iPod brought in nearly half of Apple's revenue in 2005 and dominated the marketplace in a way that caused Jobs to worry. One of his biggest fears was that an electronic device with broader applications could replace the iPod. That future threat was the cell phone. Jobs realized that he needed to develop the iPhone, which incorporated a cell phone and a music player into one device—and he needed to do it quickly. The emerging problem crystallized quickly in his mind.

His problem-solving habit was straightforward. First, he ensured that he had a strong personal and overpowering desire to create the new product. This personal desire would create the necessary force and harness the essential willpower to see the project through to completion. The threat of the future cell phone eclipsing the sales of his iPod device was real and provided the impetus for his strong desire. Second, Steve envisioned the "end state," or the outcome of the product that would make it distinctly better than its predecessors. This vision helped crystallize how all the smaller tasks and moving pieces would need to come together for the final product. Third, Jobs identified the key challenges that would need to be resolved.

Steve Jobs was remarkable at identifying the key features that would be needed and then highlighted the challenges that would need solutions. Fourth, Steve used his personal network to find and leverage the world-class practitioners who were needed to solve the specific problem at hand. If Steve could not tap into their expertise, he would buy out the company or replicate their technological prowess with other world-class performers. Fifth, Steve orchestrated the end-to-end design with ruthless focus to make the best possible product.

Steve Jobs's habit of problem solving was repeatable. To a certain degree, the problem-solving habit can be described as a sort of playbook to follow when the problem seemed to be overwhelming or insurmountable.

> Don't let the noise of others' opinions
> drown out your own inner voice.
> —Steve Jobs

In solving his problems, Steve Jobs did not rely on marketing surveys to steer his choices for consumers. Jobs trusted in own intuition and gut instincts. He believed that the consumer wasn't always sure what was possible when it came to technology. Jobs believed that most consumers would come to his products once they saw what was possible. As an entrepreneur, he learned to trust his own instincts and envision what was possible—and then go out and make it happen in the marketplace.

Bold visions require a strong will and ingrained problem-solving habits. Making the iPhone a reality would challenge the will of any strong leader, and Jobs was up to the challenge. To do so, Steve would need the cutting-edge skills of leading manufacturers in the cell phone industry, he would need simpler technology than the rotating wheel to access hundreds of songs, and he would need remarkable innovation to make it all miniaturized, compatible, and sleek. Several breakthroughs would be needed to realize this vision.

Multitouch Screen

Challenge 1 was the sleek visual display that could provide customers with detailed choices for both phone and music. Steve Jobs, with the help of Jony Ive, was able to connect the dots with a multitouch screen capability that Apple had been developing for the MacBook Pro.[28] Later, Apple discovered a small firm named FingerWorks that was experimenting with a number of multitouch trackpads for the electronics industry. Two researchers at the University of Delaware, Wayne Westerman and John Elias, had developed patents for how to translate finger moves, such as wipes and pinches, into actual functions on a keyboard screen. Within short order, Apple quickly bought out the company—with the entire suite of patents and the innovative skills of the two academics.[29]

Gorilla Glass

Challenge 2 was the need to develop a new translucent material that was stronger than plastic and resistant to scratches. Steve Jobs firmly believed that the feel of glass would be more elegant and more substantive to the delicate touch of consumers. On the advice of a friend, John Seeley Brown—a board member of the of Corning Glass—Jobs decided to call the company's CEO, Wendell Weeks,[30] and described the type of glass he needed for the iPhone. Weeks responded that Corning had developed a process in the 1960s that led to "gorilla glass." Since there was no market at the time, Corning stopped making it.

After listening to Weeks lecturing him on the making of "gorilla glass," Steve became an instant fan. He asked how much gorilla glass Corning could produce in six months and was told that none of Corning's plants make the glass at that time.

Steve Jobs replied, "Yes, you can do it. Get your mind around it."[31]

Corning Glass made the effort. Weeks said, "We did it in under six months...and we produced a glass that had never been made."[32]

Razor-Thin Device

Challenge 3 was to have the sleek design of a world-class cell phone. Steve Jobs complained to Ive's design team that the problem with the initial iPhone design was that the bulky aluminum case competed with the beauty of the display. It looked too masculine. When others would have gone ahead, Jobs pressed the pause button on the iPhone project. "Guys, you've killed yourselves over this design for the last nine months, but we're going to change it."[33] Steve added, "We're all going to work nights and weekends...and if you want we can hand out some guns so you can kill us now."[34] The design team worked until the razor-thin design was achieved. The new iPhone became the thinnest smartphone on the market, and the screen dominated the entire device.

Critics will always be out there. For every original innovator, there are probably a dozen critics. The significant difference between Jobs and others was that he developed his inner compass and his ability to solve problems. With an inspired focus on the needs of the customer, Jobs pursued excellence in spite of the critics. By following the instincts of his inner compass and problem-solving habits, he was able to pursue excellence for the iPhone. He used his strong will to overcome obstacles to the iPhone product.

You can also benefit from developing strong problem-solving habits. In every career path, there are always problems that need to be solved. Embrace the challenge and reap the benefits of strong problem-solving habits.

Habit of Character: Innovate by Connecting the Dots

Innovation comes from people meeting up in the hallways or calling each other at 10:30 at night with a new idea, or because they realized something that shoots holes in how we've been thinking about a problem. It's ad hoc meetings of six people called by someone who thinks he has figured out the coolest new thing ever and who wants to know what other people think of his idea.

—Steve Jobs

Creativity is just connecting things. When you ask creative people how they did something, they feel a little guilty because they didn't really do it, they just saw something. It seemed obvious to them after a while.

—Steve Jobs

Steve Jobs was a master of innovation. A survey of his products revealed this deep-seated habit of innovation. Innovation exuded from everything Jobs touched, and it was apparent in his basic approach. Innovation was a key part of his character. His innovative skills became the very fabric of who Jobs was and affected his thinking processes to a high degree. The lens of innovation influenced who he was and who he became in his career.

Innovation was a part of his thought process and part of his mind-set. To understand the process of innovation, we must provide an example of Steve Jobs's methods. One of the techniques of innovation that Jobs mastered was innovating in the boundaries between two separate fields of an industry. Jobs characterized this form of innovation as "connecting the dots."

You can't connect the dots looking forward; you can only connect them looking backward. So you have to trust that the dots will somehow connect in your future. You have to trust in something—your gut, destiny, life, karma, whatever. This approach has

never let me down, and it has made all
the difference in my life.

—Steve Jobs

One of the greatest impacts that Steve Jobs created
was finding an innovation that spanned two separate fields
of expertise. In this case, it was music and computer electronics. Traditionally, some of the greatest breakthroughs
in innovation occur between the boundaries of two fields
of expertise. The internal combustion engine and the
horse-bound carriage led to the explosion of the automo-
bile industry. The advent of the electrical current and the
appropriate lighting filaments of Thomas Edison created
the light industry. Marconi's radio waves coupled with the
diode vacuum tube screens combined to form the foundation of television industry across extremely long distances.

Steve Jobs was one of those rare individuals who
exploited the merger of two separate fields of expertise to
create the next level of consumer experience. Steve was a
latecomer to the merger between music and computers.
In the 1990s, there was an explosion of various digital
sound formats to store and play music on personal computers. Numerous start-up companies played with "jukebox" applications to handle the MP3 devices with their
compressed forms of digital music. Entrepreneurs began
to record audio tracks from their compact discs directly
onto their computers. Eventually, this led to explorers who
wanted to create a business model for music companies to
sell directly to individual consumers.

Napster broke the mold in the 1990s. A Massachusetts
teenager, Shawn Fanning, developed a software applica-

tion that allowed individuals to create their own playlists of music and then share the files with other individuals around the globe. In this digital form, the music was virtually indistinguishable from the original recordings. *Pirating* music became widespread with the rapid spread of Napster applications. Without appropriate controls in place, this illegal activity almost ruined the music industry.

Steve Jobs began to realize that the merger of consumer electronics and the computer industry was a huge growth market in the making. However, Apple was late to the game since a large number of small companies had already developed software to handle music management. Real Jukebox, Windows Media Player, and a variant of Hewlett Packard were already on the market. However, these second-rate products lacked the quality that most people desired.

One key leadership technique is that if you're far behind in the technology game, seek a company to buy that is already at the cutting edge in the game. At the time, three developers had created "jukebox" applications for the Macintosh computer. Of the group, Steve found a particular liking for the application called SoundJam. Two former Apple software developers, Jeff Robbin and Dave Keller, had created it. One key advantage to SoundJam was its highly refined database program, which allowed it to file music recordings according to more than a dozen attributes. Filing would be critically important since some users saved thousands of songs on their computers. SoundJam was also favored since it was simple to navigate, easy to operate, and able to compress recordings to much smaller digital file sizes.

Steve Jobs bought SoundJam in 2000. The other entrepreneurial technique of Jobs was to keep the take-over a secret until the software bugs had been worked out. He also ensured that every single author of the SoundJam program would come to work for Apple. By doing so, he made certain that the competition would not gain any advantage from former employers of SoundJam. Jobs would keep the takeover secret for more than two years to allow the SoundJam product to be fully compatible with iTunes. Steve prevented further leaks by threatening employees that any leaks to other companies would result in being fired from Apple. With close oversight, Steve transformed SoundJam into an Apple product.

Jobs announced the advent of iTunes in 2001. Keeping with the Apple brand, it embraced simplicity with a sleek brushed-metal finish. The device reduced the query features to allow just a simple box to type in the characteristic of a song, whether it was an album, a song, or an artist's name. iTunes became a part of the digital hub strategy and was free to all Mac users. With the recognition of a merging of the music industry and the computer industry, Jobs took the lead of the wave of innovations through quick thinking and rapid modifications of the handheld devices. This habit of innovation continued through Steve's successful application of "connecting the dots."

A lot of people in our industry haven't had very diverse experiences. So they don't have enough dots to connect, and they end up with very linear solutions without a broad perspective on the problem. The broader one's understanding of the human experience, the better design we will have.

—Steve Jobs

The Emergence of the iPod

The advent of the iPod was a product of connecting the dots. Steve Jobs was a master at innovation and connecting the dots. Following the development of the iTunes product, the next step in Steve's digital hub strategy was the creation of a portable music player device. Steve recognized the unique opportunity to bring out a simpler device coupled with the iTunes software program. He also realized that competitors in this field were substandard for customers.

Steve Jobs loved music. He held great passion for music player devices, and as a consumer, he came to the conclusion that the current devices on the market "truly sucked."[35] All of Steve's advisers, including Jon Rubinstein and Phil Schiller and the remainder of the iTunes team, agreed. Phil Schiller played around with the other music players and stated, "These things really stink. You couldn't figure out to use them...and [they] only held about sixteen songs."[36] The Apple team saw an opportunity to make a truly revolutionary product.

Steve Jobs put pressure on his engineers to develop a portable music player in 2000. Jon Rubinstein, an Apple engineer, was a key figure in this development. Rubinstein did a survey of the key components and identified a small LCD screen and lithium battery that would work. In his opinion, not all of the required components were ready for a great player. The greatest obstacle was the need for a suitable disk drive, which would need to be extremely small but have the memory of a superior music player. Without this great memory ability, the music players would continue to be mediocre.

Jon Rubinstein helped connect the dots for Steve Jobs. People who connect the dots must be aware of the environment and the gaps, and they must seek the missing pieces in a completely new environment. At an ordinary supplier meeting in Japan, Rubinstein saw a tiny 1.8-inch drive at Toshiba that could hold five gigabytes of data. It was about the size of a silver dollar. Five gigabytes was able to hold about "a thousand songs."[37] At that moment, Rubinstein saw a flash of the possibilities. Jobs was at the Tokyo MacWorld conference in Japan. Jon visited Jobs at the Hotel Okura and said, "All I need is a $10 million check," to make the new music player work. With a quick authorization, Steve Jobs was on his way to creating a revolutionary music player. The breakthrough came about by connecting the dots with a key component of the device: a simple 1.8-inch drive.

Tony Fadell was selected to put the iPod together. Fadell was a programmer who had started three companies on his own. He had specialized in creating handheld devices at General Magic and Philips Electronics. Fadell had even created his own version of a great MP3 player to market to RealNetworks, Palm, Sony, and Philips before being hired by Apple. With his expertise, he was able to package the various components of the Toshiba disk drive, the screen, the battery, and the packaging to create the magical iPod. Creating the iPod was undoubtedly a team effort, but the secret sauce of innovation came about through connecting the dots of entrepreneurial talent, key components, and consumer market demand for a revolutionary music player product.

Innovation by connecting the dots was a derivation of both a mind-set and a habit. Steve Jobs mastered this habit of innovation. He recognized that connecting the dots was more than identifying unique relationships and was part of a chain of connections. Steve was able to "find the new dots" through strategic partnerships with those who had specialized expertise in a field in which he needed information.

Without finding these new dots, his thinking would have been limited to in-house expertise—and Apple would not have been able to make the grand breakthroughs that were essential in the field. Finding a new dot with the Corning Corporation led to the breakthrough of Google Glass, which was essential to the iPhone's success. Steve "catalogued the dots" in a way that he could quickly and easily access the dots to help him solve a problem. Steve found a way to network the dots based on the innovative approach that he took to solve problems. Each approach used a different combination of dots that was unique to his approach.

You can learn to innovate in a similar manner. You can refine your ability to find new insights, catalogue them, network ideas, and organize the ideas into a coherent picture that leads to significant innovation.

Habit of Character: Purveyor of Big Ideas

When you grow up you tend to get told the world is the way it is and…to live your life inside the world. Try not to bash into the walls too much. Try to have a nice family, have fun, save a little money. That's a very limited life. Life can be much broader once you discover one simple fact: Everything around you that you call life was made up by people that were no smarter than you and you can change it, you can influence it, you can build your own things that other people can use. Once you learn that, you'll never be the same again.

—Steve Jobs

I want to put a ding in the universe.

—Steve Jobs

Even though Jobs was a relatively obscure figure in the 1970s, he had big dreams for the future of computing. At the time, International Business Machines (IBM) dominated the field. In the 1970s, computers consisted of large mainframe computers that took huge rooms to store the guts of the machinery. It was highly impersonal with the individual workstations linked to this huge machinery. It was uncomfortable. Workers had to manage their information with batch cards that were sterile, laborious, painstaking to manage, and extremely cumbersome. Later, workers were wedded to small workstation terminals that were located in the same building as the mainframe computers. Individuals could not work at home or in remote locations away from the gargantuan computers. These work conditions were stifling, uncomfortable, and personally inhibiting. It lacked a personal touch.

> I've always been attracted to the more revolutionary changes. I don't know why. Because they're harder. They're much more stressful emotionally. And you usually go through a period where everybody tells you that you've completely failed.
>
> —Steve Jobs

Steve Jobs had a bold vision for the advent of the personal computer. He knew what computer operators desired and what would work with the average family household. With Steve Wozniak's creation of the chip within a small circuit board with the power of expansion, Jobs began to realize that this device could completely transform the future of computers and change the lifestyle of the American household. What would happen if a stay-at-home homemaker could wake up to a cup of coffee and access a personal computer that could manage his or her information for the day? The average homemaker could get the daily news, check stock prices, manage the household budget, and access daily to-do lists.

The personal computer fit nicely with the spirit of the entrepreneurs in

California. Filled with the free spirit of
the age of Woodstock, the counterculture
revolution of the post-Beatles period,
the free lifestyle of academics on the
Pacific coast, and the waves of spiritual
freedom from Berkeley, the time was
ripe for a radical change to the age of
computers.

Computers themselves, and software
yet to be developed, will revolutionize the
way we learn.

—Steve Jobs

Steve Jobs envisioned a bold vision of the average
household having a personal computer, and it came to fruition. He thought of the personal computer as an extension of the individual and was convinced that an individual
could be transformed through the use of the computer. It
would be capable of sparking great creativity. Every creative
task that could be imagined would be able to be achieved,
and the personal computer would serve as the hub for
innovation. Music, media, videos, movies, graphic designs,
computational calculations, architecture, paintings, and
any conceivable skill or task could be initiated, refined,
and perfected through these devices. In the end, Steve conceived of a bold idea, and it came to pass.

Steve's aspirations did not end with the personal
computer. He went on to envision the iPod, iMac,
iTunes, and iPhone, which revolutionized the way people live around the world. By embracing the notion of
purveying big ideas, you could also develop an enduring

habit of thinking beyond the possibilities of today and bringing about a vision for tomorrow.

Habit of Character: Exude a Positive Attitude and Develop Determination to Make a Difference

> Bottom line is, I didn't return to Apple to make a fortune. I've been very lucky in my life and already have one. When I was twenty-five, my net worth was $100 million or so. I decided then that I wasn't going to let it ruin my life. There's no way you could ever spend it all, and I don't view wealth as something that validates my intelligence.
>
> —Steve Jobs

Steve Jobs embraced and exuded a positive attitude in everything he did. Whether it involved rebounding from leaving Apple in 1985, dealing with terminal cancer, or having to start at ground zero with a new business, Steve epitomized the kind of individual who exuded a positive attitude in spite of all of life's difficulties. At the core of this habit was his foundational outlook on life. Steve believed that he was special and marked for great distinction in his life. He instinctively knew that he would make a difference and literally spent the rest of his life "making a dent" in the universe.

Entrepreneur Mark Cuban also realized the value of a positive attitude and personal determination. A lesson he learned in his twenties involved this determination.

DR. ROBERT M. TOGUCHI

He discovered that "with time and effort [he] could learn any new technology that was released."[38] When an entrepreneur hits a period of setbacks, the competition isn't going to slow down. However, with determination, you can accelerate past the competitors because of the skills and knowledge you acquire. Mark Cuban observed that he was able to beat the so-called experts in the IT sector because he was willing to put the effort into knowing more than the competition. To Steve, money was important—but it wasn't the primary consideration in business. Money does a lot of things. It opens doors. It creates choices that may not be available otherwise. Money keeps the production line going, but it doesn't buy happiness or ensure job satisfaction. The intangibles that money did not provide were much more important to Steve.

When it comes to money, Steve quoted one of Mike Markkula's key principles. He noted that Mike Markkula emphasized, "You should never start a company with the goal of getting rich. Your goal should be making something you believe in and making a company that will last." That great advice helped Steve with his decision to return to Apple. His comeback had very little to do with money, and it had a lot to do with rejuvenating Apple into a company that would last. The habit of positive thinking can be contagious, and it can permeate the way you live your life.

Habit of Character: Relentless Focus

> That's been one of my mantras—focus and simplicity. Simple can be harder

than complex; you have to work hard to get your thinking clean to make it simple.

—Steve Jobs

Steve Job has been known for his unparalleled ability to focus. Whether in the boardroom, his personal life, or his ability to gain partners for his business, Steve had an uncanny ability to focus. He brought focus to his meetings, his product reviews, his product lines, and the boardroom. In every way, uncommon and relentless focus was the hallmark of Steve's distinct leadership style, and it made a monumental difference in his ability to execute projects of great complexity. He always made it look simple.

Focus is critical to any leader. It separates average leaders from the world-class leaders who take large companies to the next level of success. Thomas Edison, Bill Gates, Jeff Bezos, Elon Musk, and Mark Cuban belong in the category of remarkable leaders who distinguished themselves through unparalleled ability to focus.

Focus unclutters the details. Under the leadership of CEO Gil Amelio, Apple floundered in the midst of clutter. Scores of diverse projects associated with mediocre technologies crowded the product line of the Apple corporation. With this clutter, the direction of Apple's engineering expertise was characterized by haphazardness, minutia, and unfocused leadership. The brilliance of focus is that it brings order, provides direction, picks the winners, and organizes teams to bring about product excellence through attention to detail. Steve completely turned Apple around through determination, discipline, and uncommon focus.

Reality Distortion Field

Steve Jobs had the ability to apply focus on those around him. Close associates of Steve describe the phenomenon as the reality distortion field.[39]

Bud Tribble, a software developer on the Macintosh team, said, "Steve has a reality distortion field... In his presence, reality is malleable. He can convince anyone of practically anything. It wears off when he's not around, but it makes it hard to have realistic schedules."[40]

Another member of the Macintosh team, Andy Hertzfeld, also became acutely aware of Steve's unusual ability to focus and distort reality around him. Hertzfeld stated, "The reality distortion field was a confounding mélange of a charismatic rhetorical style, indomitable will, and eagerness to bend any fact to fit the purpose at hand." Steve would imagine and set incredibly impossible goals and expect the team to meet his unusual expectations. One example was Steve's desire to complete the creation of the Macintosh system by January 1982 in less than a year. The software developers clearly noted that "that's crazy," but reality did not stop Steve from imagining the impossible.

Debi Coleman, another team member, described the reality distortion focus as almost being "hypnotized." She claimed that Steve "reminded me of Rasputin...he laser-beamed in on you and didn't blink. It didn't matter if he was serving purple Kool-Aid. You drank it."[41] Steve's ability to focus was to a certain degree "empowering." With his ability to demand the impossible, Steve could inspire his Macintosh team to literally change the previous computer benchmarks of what was possible. Debi noted, "You did the impossible because you didn't realize it was impossible." How many of us have worked for a demanding leader who stretched the art of the possible by moving the goalposts? Steve mastered the ability of focusing himself and others in the enterprises through his remarkable ability to distort reality for an impossible outcome.

Later, in his return to Apple, Steve Jobs used his uncanny focus to improve his management abilities as the interim CEO, or iCEO. While Jobs had demonstrated his clear abilities as a creative genius and a visionary, he had not mastered the ability to run a company. During his first tour at Apple, he had unmistakably demonstrated that he had not mastered that skill. Now at the second turn, he was able to display a keen sense of detailed focus and management. Steve Jobs focused on the bottom line. Wasteful projects were eliminated. Jobs took a scalpel to cut express product lines from Apple's core business. He also cut unneeded software features in the new operating system for the Apple under development. Jobs also took a hard look on the need to maintain control over production within Apple factories. Instead, he shifted toward outsourcing as many of the manufacturing lines as possible to outside suppliers.

He demanded rigorous discipline on Apple suppliers. They either met their requirements or were let go.

When Jobs took over as iCEO, Apple kept more than two months' supplies of Apple computers on hand, literally more than any other tech company. To Jobs, this was unacceptable. When he found that Airborne Express, a supplier, wasn't delivering spare parts on time, he ordered an Apple manager to sever the contract. Instead of obeying, the Apple manager noted that Airborne Express would start a lawsuit. Jobs did not budge. He said, "If they…with us, [you tell them] they'll never get another…dime from this company ever."[42] The Apple manager quit under the pressure. Nonetheless, Steve got the results he desired. The new supplier of spare parts was ordered to cut inventory by 75 percent, and it did. Focus led to results.

Jobs had a vision of bringing Apple inventory under control and moving toward "just-in-time manufacturing." To get there, he hired a thirty-seven-year-old procurement and supply chain manager named Tim Cook. Both were familiar with what was possible, and Tim Cook shared Jobs's vision to bring about ruthless discipline to the supply process.

Tim Cook was a supply chain manager from Compaq computers. A son of a shipyard worker, Tim came from a small town in Alabama. With an industrial engineering degree from Auburn University and a business degree from Duke University, he also had twelve years of experience working for IBM in the Research Triangle Park in North Carolina. A very logical engineer, Tim Cook brought discipline to the manufacturing processes at Apple.

Tim Cook was diligent and focused at his work. A bachelor without family responsibilities, Tim devoted himself completely to his work at Apple to bring focus to the team. Getting up early, he started sending e-mails at four thirty, exercised for an hour at the gym, and arrived at Apple by six. Truly focused, he set Sunday evening conference calls with his team to set conditions for the entire week. With discipline and focus, Tim Cook helped Apple cut its key suppliers from one hundred to twenty-four and shut down ten of Apple's nineteen warehouses to implement Steve's vision of just-in-time manufacturing and delivery processes. With Steve's direction, Tim Cook reduced inventory from two months' worth of products down to one month's inventory in the early months of 1998. By September 1998, he reduced the inventory to six days. By September 1999, inventory got down to a remarkable two days of supply. He demonstrated what focus can do to a cutting-edge company. The habit of focus can pay large dividends to any enterprise. The ability to incorporate the habit of relentless focus to your daily routine can also have a significant impact on your effectiveness in your career.

Habit of Character: Nurture the Spirit of Perseverance

> I'm convinced that about half of what separates successful entrepreneurs from the non-successful ones is pure perseverance.
> —Steve Jobs

Show me a man who is diligent in his work, and I will show you a successful man. In today's society, the ingrained habit of perseverance is a rarity. How often do you see or observe those who are willing to go the extra mile at work? When workers discover that they are the last ones at the office, do they run out the door or do the little things that are necessary to bring about success? Is perseverance a habit, a daily routine, or an afterthought that occurs on rare occasions?

The habit of perseverance is unusual. Finding an individual who truly dedicates himself or herself to overcoming insurmountable obstacles in all walks of life on a routine basis is uncommon. Going the extra mile when no one else is around to watch is a habit that places an individual in a different class of employees at any firm. Yet this is one of the priceless habits that Steve possessed without even thinking about it. It was ingrained, and it happened routinely. Over time, this unusual habit made Jobs incredibly successful.

Steve Jobs displayed perseverance in the perfection of his product presentations. The rollout of the Apple Macintosh in 1984 exemplified the value of perseverance to get the presentation environment delivery to a high state of perfection. Like all of his other launches, Steve did not leave any detail to chance. Leading up to the actual event, he ensured that Apple sponsored a television ad and managed to arrange a series of press interviews with *Newsweek* and *Rolling Stone*. Then for the actual launch experience in the Flint Auditorium of De Anza Community College, Steve would put on the special touches that led to excellence.

Steve placed great emphasis on the atmospherics. Eight days before the launch—on January 24, 1984—Steve came up with a new idea. He stated, "We need a demo for the intro!"[43] He described his vision of adding a touch of dramatics by showing off the features of the Macintosh with the inspirational theme from *Chariots of Fire*. They only had a few days to put it together.

Andy Hertzfeld and the team agreed that it would be "fun to cook up something impressive." In addition to the *Chariots of Fire* background music, Steve wanted the Macintosh to be the first computer to introduce itself. All of this had to be programmed on a computer on short order. The stage lighting also needed to be perfect. With great enthusiasm, Steve insisted on John Sculley being the detailed judge of small variations in the lightning. With constant adjustments to the lighting, John Sculley was ordered from seat to seat with varying angles to the stage to critique the accompanying shades of light that were needed for the perfect atmosphere for the viewers. Changes to the stage lighting and repeated rehearsals went on for five hours— well into the night before the performance. The session included changes to the font displays, drawings, charts, and additional pictures of a thought bubble encapsulating a Macintosh computer.

In the end, Steve created the atmospherics and environment that he wanted for the perfect unveiling of the Macintosh. It certainly exceeded expectations. In all of this, his efforts revealed that perseverance in the delivery of a product had its benefits. Not everyone has it, but Steve displayed an unusual amount of perseverance as a habit.

Habit of Character: Embrace Boldness and Audacity

Have the courage to follow your heart and intuition. They somehow already know what you truly want to become. Everything else is secondary.

—Steve Jobs

Everyone here has the sense that right now is one of those moments when we are influencing the future.

—Steve Jobs

Boldness

It has been said that the killer of dreams coming true is a lack of courage.[44] Several factors can prevent emerging leaders and entrepreneurs from pursuing their dreams. One of the prevailing factors is the inherent fear of the unknown or the hidden pitfalls when one pursues his or her dream. Fear can paralyze one's ability to make decisions or take action, and it can hinder one's initiative to reach out for that dream. Second, naysayers—whether family members, friends, or business associates—can have a dampening effect on realizing one's dreams. History is replete with those who succumbed to the counsel of their fears and missed their opportunity for greatness in their field. It must be realized that true greatness is rarely achieved by those who lack boldness and courage in their convictions.

Steve Jobs was different. Unlike others, he displayed unusual boldness and audacity at an early age. In September 1971, when he was just sixteen years old, Steve partnered with his close friend Stephen Wozniak on a bold venture. One Sunday afternoon, Wozniak read an *Esquire* article that his mother had left on the table. Wozniak was getting ready to head off to Berkeley for college when he became mesmerized with the technical piece. "Secrets of the Little Blue Box" by Ron Rosenbaum[45] told of how hackers had found innovative ways to make a long-distance call for free. It involved mimicking the high-pitched frequencies on the AT&T network that were used to route signals. Could this be true?

Wozniak knew that Jobs would fall in love with the idea in the article. Halfway through reading it, Wozniak called Jobs at home and starting reading every word over the phone. One of the heroes in the article was John Draper, a fellow hacker who realized that the sound made by toy whistles could replicate the same tone used by the call-routing switches over the AT&T phone network. By repeating the high-pitched tones, John Draper described how his little technique could literally fool the AT&T system into making long-distance phone calls for free. Draper's discovery was amazing. Moreover, the article told about how the related tones to route calls could be located by reading the issue of the *Bell System Technical Journal.*

Jobs didn't hesitate. He absolutely knew that they needed to get their hands on the journal that day. Wozniak decided to drive, and they headed to the Stanford Linear Accelerator Center Library. Even though it was Sunday and the library was closed, Steve Jobs found a way. By sneaking through a door that was usually left opened, Wozniak and Jobs scoured through the aisles and searched feverishly for the technical journal. Wozniak was the first to find it. With amazement, Wozniak and Jobs realized that the designated frequencies and their impact were real. They were beside themselves.

Without a moment's delay, Wozniak and Jobs raced to the Sunnyvale Electronics store to buy the parts for building an analog tone generator. Using his experience in building frequency counters, Jobs used a simple dial to mimic and tape record the tones that were listed in the *Bell System Technical Journal.* When it came close to midnight, they were ready to try it. Unfortunately for the two adventurers, the oscillators were not quite stable enough to precisely replicate the high frequencies needed to fool the AT&T system. They just couldn't make it work that night. But true to their calling, they didn't give up. Wozniak committed himself to creating a digital version of the tone generator once he returned to Berkeley.

The digital version of the blue box had not been created before. Wozniak remained undeterred. Patching together transistors and diodes on his circuit board, Wozniak built the first digital blue box before Thanksgiving. He was thoroughly impressed with the design he had created. Something marvelous and new was in Wozniak's hands for the next step. Instead of testing it out on his own, Wozniak drove down to Jobs's house for the trial run.

Their first call was to Steve Wozniak's uncle in Los Angeles. Rather than connecting with their uncle, they dialed an unknown caller. It didn't matter. The long-distance call had gone through. It worked. Their bold invention had made it through the maze of chirps necessary to fool AT&T. They had achieved a small miracle. This bold venture proved that Jobs and Wozniak could partner on a technology project with a high payoff and real prospects for success. This small taste of a little victory was only the beginning of the Apple legend they would both create.

Boldness can be nurtured. Boldness can be developed. To many, boldness can be an outgrowth of personal conviction. When one is convinced that a better way is possible, a deep personal conviction can become the overriding concern that surpasses fear and takes one down new paths. With conviction, boldness and audacity can become ingrained habits.

Habit of Character: Be Able to Get Along with People

> Technology is nothing. What's important is that you have a faith in people, that they're basically good and smart, and if you give them tools, they'll do wonderful things with them.
>
> —Steve Jobs

Steve did not always get along with people. This was a learned habit. His initial impression on other people was often unimpressive. One of his early mentors, Mike Markkula, recalls how Steve habitually made poor impressions on clients and other workers. In 1977, Mike noted that Steve would regularly not take showers and needed deodorant.[46] With his vegan diet, Steve believed that he could forego the basics of hygiene due to his special dietary restrictions. Steve would enter meetings with bare feet, and fellow workers would complain about having to look at his dirty feet.

Steve's personal appearance was generally appalling, and some even thought he resembled Ho Chi Minh. With habits like these, first impressions would consistently be a problem. Over time, Steve developed the habit of making a great first impression. Along with these skills, Steve also learned the art of wooing high-profile individuals over to Apple. One such case occurred when Steve sought the expert advice of John Sculley, then the president of the Pepsi-Cola division of PepsiCo in New York. Through the counsel of Gerry Roche, a corporate headhunter, Steve discovered that John Sculley was the creator of the Pepsi Challenge campaign, which was a remarkable advertising success for Pepsi.

Steve learned the habit of turning on the charm. For Steve, making a great first impression focused on the client atmosphere. To set the conditions for John Sculley, Steve invited him to a restaurant at the Four Seasons. Steve's dinner conversation inspired John Sculley with the vision and possibility of designing a marketing campaign to create a whole Apple generation of loyal fans and supporters. Capitalizing on the advent of personal computers, John was wooed to be a central figure in creating this national movement of excitement. John had a unique opportunity to make history. Steve's charm had a lasting impact on John Sculley, so much so, that he continued to think about Apple's potential at his Greenwich, Connecticut, home for several days after his West Coast visit. Steve developed the habit of influencing people.

Steve also developed the ability to connect with people on a deep personal level. Jobs took the time to learn everything about people he sought to impress. In the case of John Sculley, Steve learned that John loved art. To turn on the charm, Steve took walks with John through Central Park. He also took a stroll with John to the Metropolitan Museum of Art to observe and discuss Periclean sculptures, Greek and Roman figures of antiquity. After learning that John took his vacations to Paris to draw sketches of the

Seine River, Steve replied that he could "see himself as a poet in Paris."[47] Steve encouraged John to relate to him on a personal level.

Later, Sculley observed, "I gained a sense that I could be a teacher to a brilliant student... I saw in him a mirror image of my younger self."[48] It was obvious that Steve had learned the important habit of making a personal connection and getting along with people. With skill, he inspired Sculley to embrace a unique mentorship role, which was an outgrowth of a personal bond that was formed. Later in their careers, both Sculley and Jobs would experience a falling out in their relationship due to a downturn in Apple's sales. Nonetheless, at their first meeting, Steve had demonstrated the ability to connect on a deep personal level with Sculley. He had mastered the habits of making a superb first impression and influencing people.

Mark Cuban, owner of the Dallas Mavericks, testifies to the importance of getting along with people. Over his career, Mark recognized the value of being people savvy. In his mind, an entrepreneur has got to become a people person if he or she wants to build an empire. He noted, "People hate dealing with people who are jerks...it's always easier to be nice than to be a jerk. Don't be a jerk."[49] Those who intend to develop a successful following must learn to get along with people. Without a doubt, learning how to get along with people will provide an important stepping-stone toward greater success.

Habit of Character: Internalize the Habit of Bouncing Back from Failure

> Getting fired from Apple was the best thing that could have ever happened to me. The heaviness of being successful was replaced by the lightness of being a beginner again. It freed me to enter one of the most creative periods of my life.
>
> —Steve Jobs

> Sometimes life's going to hit you in the head with a brick. Don't lose faith. I'm convinced that the only thing that kept me going was that I loved what I did.
>
> —Steve Jobs

Steve Jobs mastered the art of bouncing back. Interestingly, many successful billionaires have tasted the setback of failure. Donald Trump, Walt Disney, and Mark Cuban all experienced financial difficulties and had short periods of personal business turmoil. Their recoveries served as a testament to their character, perseverance, and belief in themselves. Jobs was not an exception. Although he experienced the rapid rise to wealth and fame with his development and marketing of the Apple II and Macintosh, Jobs was removed as CEO of Apple in 1985 after a showdown with John Sculley.

The setback for Steve Jobs was ugly. Despite the rapid rise of Apple's innovation with the Apple II and the Macintosh, insiders within Apple sought to remove Jobs from his operational role in the company. John Sculley, the Apple CEO, was not impressed with the running of the Macintosh division and viewed Steve as a threat to his leadership role within Apple. At the heart of the disagreement was a clash in the personalities of Steve and John Sculley.

Steve Jobs, the intellectual founder of Apple, valued the quality of the product that his company provided to the computer industry. In his mind, the leader of Apple needed to have a deep appreciation for the quality of its products. Steve was very sensitive to the little things that made Apple a great brand. He spent time with software compatibility, product look, speed of execution, and other important design characteristics. Steve wanted to improve the affordability of the Macintosh line, looking at ways to cut component costs and reduce the overall cost to the average consumer.

John Sculley, on the other hand, was not a strong advocate for the nuances of the Apple product line. John grew up in his financial career by selling sodas and snack foods. Not surprisingly, he did not show any interest in the details of the recipes since it was not important to him. The bottom line to Sculley was maximizing profits, and he did not spend the time to learn about the details of his products. This lack of interest bothered Steve. It was unconscionable for the CEO to not grasp the details of Apple's core products.

John Sculley criticized the way Steve ran the Macintosh division. In March 1985, sales for the Macintosh computer were dropping—and met only 10 percent of the sales forecast. Scully used the anemic sales and internal complaints about Jobs's harsh behavior with his workforce to call for his removal from the Macintosh division. To lure Steve away from his leadership position, several team members proposed that Steve create a small team to design and develop new products for Apple. Although Steve had a personal interest in a skunkwork facility, he was not going to be pushed out of his leadership role. Steve fought back and plotted a coup to remove John Sculley from his CEO position.

At an executive staff meeting in May 1985, John Sculley confronted Steve on his plot to remove him from the company. Instead of backing down, Jobs claimed that he would do a better job in running Apple than John Sculley in front of the executive committee. Sculley called for a vote. One by one, each of the board members, including Regis McKenna, Del Yocam, Al Eisenstat, and Bill Campbell, voted against Steve. The vote was unanimous. Jobs was removed from the Macintosh, and it was probably the lowest point in Steve's career. In September 1985, Steve resigned from Apple. At that moment, he owned 6.5 million shares of Apple stock—worth more than $100 million. Within five months, he sold all of his stock except one share. At age thirty, he would have to start over.

His comeback is well-known. Without hesitation, Steve began to plan his way forward to success. He used his ingrained habits of character, knowledge, and execution to make a new path as a leading entrepreneur in the electronics industry. First, with the start-up with NeXT and then with the establishment of Pixar, Jobs forged ahead without hesitation and without looking back. He spent time with his family and matured as a CEO beyond anyone's imagination or expectation at the time. Pixar became a blockbuster company, and NeXT was sought after by Apple. Within a short period, Apple asked its original founder to return as a senior adviser in December 1996. In the fall of 1997, Steve Jobs took over leadership of Apple as iCEO.

Setbacks in life are inevitable. People will experience periods of personal success, triumphs, and achievements that will bring great satisfaction. However, they will also have their fair share of difficulties, challenging circumstances, financial setbacks, and just plain bad luck. These setbacks are just a part of life. During those times, your personal outlook, sheer will, and confidence in your ability to weather the storm will become more important. You can overcome the difficulties of life with the right attitude and perseverance. Steve Jobs learned how to orchestrate a comeback after the humiliation of being fired from Apple. You can also learn the habit of rebounding to success.

CHAPTER 3

Habits of Knowledge

K nowing what to know is a habit. Steve Jobs realized that knowledge, skills, and attributes were extremely important to gaining success as an entrepreneur. Especially early in his career, Steve was reliant on other people's expertise to get started and began taking the first steps toward realizing his vision. He lacked the knowledge of how to develop a business plan, how to market a product, and how to develop the brand for his revolutionary product. The following discussion of habits is important for highlighting that knowledge is extremely important to being successful.

Habit of Knowledge: Think Different

Here's to the crazy ones, the misfits, the rebels, the troublemakers, the round pegs in the square holes... The ones who see things differently—they're not fond of rules... You can quote them, disagree with them, glorify or vilify them, but the only thing you can't do is ignore them because they change things... They push the human race forward, and while some may see them as the crazy ones, we see genius, because the ones who are crazy enough to think that they can change the world, are the ones who do.

During his early years, while he was still an unknown student, Steve thought of himself as being different. He was no ordinary child. Even at the young age of twelve, Steve set his sights high. He had wanted to build himself a frequency counter.[50] During the process of building this counter, Steve noticed that he required the purchase of a few parts from Hewlett-Packard. In those times, people didn't have unlisted phone numbers. As a person who believed he was different, Steve decided to look up Bill Hewlett, the original founder of Hewlett Packard—a computer giant in the 1960s—in the phone book. Bill answered the call and chatted with Steve for at least twenty minutes. He got Steve the parts he requested and offered Steve a job in the production plant that made frequency counters.

Steve knew that he was different. Steve thought differently. He did not think like the engineer designers at a computer firm. The creation of the iMac exemplifies Steve's ability to think differently about Apple's product line. Typical engineers try to design a computer with all the bells and whistles that make the final device unusable. Steve put on the quintessential lens of viewing products from the vantage point of the customer. In May 1998, Steve introduced the iMac, a desktop computer aimed solely at the market of the home consumer. It would be the complete package with monitor, computer, and keyboard all instantly ready to be used coming out of the box. Most importantly, it was priced for success and would sell for $1,200. At the time, no Apple computer sold for less than $2,000.

Desktop computers in 1998 were ugly. They were boxy, surrounded by cords, and wrapped in bland colors. In many ways, computers were unappealing to the average household customer since they were designed by engineers for office professionals who didn't care about the packaging or the look and feel of the desktop computer. Additionally, when they came out of the packaging, desktop computers were extremely hard to organize, set up, and use since they weren't designed for simplicity.

The iMac changed the image of the personal computer. Housed in a playful, translucent, molded casing, it resembled a household appliance from the Jetsons more than a clunky office work machine. The iMac came in bold colors such as Bondi blue with impressive sea-green blue tones. Later versions unveiled colors of blueberry, strawberry, grape, tangerine, and lime. It boasted the hardware design and microprocessor of the PowerMac G3, Apple's top-end professional computer. The device entered stores in August 1998.

Remarkably, the iMac sold more than 278,000 units in the first month and a half. By year's end, it would sell 800,000 units, thereby becoming the fastest-selling computer for Apple. Of greatest significance, 32 percent of

THE WINNING HABITS OF STEVE JOBS

iMacs sold went to first-time buyers of computers, and an additional 12 percent were sold to customers using Windows.[51] The iMac broke records for Apple and restored the company's reputation as the leader of innovation.

Steve Jobs developed habits to think differently. He was keen to emphasize that one needed a viewpoint that challenged the status quo. "Think different" required one to completely break away from past thought processes and habits to achieve new ways of understanding and embrace new ways of developing breakthroughs.[52] He believed in looking for the points that converged between two separate fields of discipline, such as the where the field of liberal arts converged with science and technology. He also thought that think different required the ability to visualize and anticipate the future by bringing the future to the present. All of these approaches were new habits of thought. Think different was a way to transform Apple into a revitalized company. You can also benefit from incorporating new habits of thought in your daily routine.

Habit of Knowledge: Knowing the Competition Can Be a Powerful Motivator

Steve Jobs was quite adept at anticipating the next step. In 2005, the iPod was soaring in terms of sales and revenue. Within that year, Apple sold more than twenty million devices and literally quadrupled the number of sales from the previous year. It was getting scary. Due to sheer volume, the iPod was affecting the bottom line of Apple's profits and reaching 45 percent of revenue generation in

81

2005. The iPod was dominating the industry and increasing the comparable sales of Mac computers.

The overwhelming success of the iPod began to create fears. At the top of their game, CEOs begin to wonder about what would come next. Was there anything out there in the marketplace that could threaten the future success of the iPod? As usual, Steve was out in front of this thinking. Steve said, "The device that can eat our lunch is the cell phone." Cell phones were everywhere. People carried cell phones to the supermarket, the mall, movie theaters, and restaurants. They were ubiquitous. They were everywhere. In 2005, more than 825 million cell phones were sold. Steve's great fear was that some manufacturer would build the music players into the next generation of cell phone. He claimed, "Everyone carries a phone, so that would render the iPod unnecessary."[53]

Steve Jobs's response to the marketplace reflected his knowledge of the competition and how the competition would adapt in the future. Wayne Gretzky stated, "I skate to where the puck is going to be—not where it has been." Steve was not interested in the current state of technology; he was more interested in where the competition was going to be in the near future. In his mind, the invention of the iPod as a handheld device would lead others to conceive of the potential to harness the power of voice communications and music in one device. If you have developed an ingrained habit of knowing the competition and their behaviors, you will have a marked advantage in the competitive space.

The first effort of building the iPod into a cell phone involved a partnership. Since Motorola had developed the

RAZR, which was a combination of a cell phone and a camera, Steve laid out a strategy to partner with Motorola. Steve wanted the RAZR to build an iPod into it and have all three features in one device. The outcome was the ROKR. The ROKR, unfortunately, had all of the features of minimalism build into the new phone. It was ugly, had a hundred-song limit, and took a long time to load.[54] All the features of a product designed by a committee were in this device.

From Jobs's point of view, it was a failure. Nonetheless, through persistence and realizing the end result of not competing, Jobs perfected the iPhone, which has dominated the marketplace. Knowing the competition can inspire anyone to strive for the next big breakthrough. Your knowledge of your key competitors in your field of expertise will provide you with the competitive edge to anticipate the next big innovation for your business.

Habit of Knowledge: Inspire and Create the Brand

Apple is about people who think outside the box, who want to use computers to help them change the world.[55]
—Steve Jobs

Steve Jobs was extremely aware of the Apple brand. It stood for something great. It was not the outcome of a few quick wins. Apple's brand was an outgrowth of decades of perseverance and a combination of high-quality purpose, remarkable innovations, unrelenting execution, and visionary products that reflected something far deeper than what the human consciousness would be able to tap into.

Jobs believed that Apple was "one of the great brands of the world, probably in the top five based on emotional appeal."[56] When Apple CEO Gil Amelio resigned from his post in July 1997, Steve saw an opportunity to capture the essence of the Apple brand in a campaign. As he put it, "We at Apple had forgotten who we were. One way to remember who you are is to remember who your heroes are. That was the genesis of that campaign."[57]

To reestablish the brand, Jobs reached out to who he considered to be the best in the field of advertising, Lee Clow, the creative director at TBWA/Chiat/Day in Los Angeles. Clow had developed the phenomenal "1984" ad campaign that launched the Macintosh. As Steve described the project to Clow, he noted, "We have to prove that Apple is still alive and that it still stands for something special."[58] Lee Clow was a huge fan of Apple. Redefining the brand would not be difficult. Clow had drunk the proverbial Apple Kool-Aid and knew and understood the quality of Steve Jobs's work. Lee Clow simply loved Apple. Before bringing Clow on board, Steve was not impressed with the presentations of a host of advertising agencies, including Arnold Worldwide and BBDO. The others simply lacked the edge that Steve was looking for.

"Think Different" was the idea that became the centerpiece of the Apple brand. Steve was beside himself. The new idea caused Steve to cry. Without a doubt, it was ten times better than anything the other agencies had developed. It appealed to Steve because of the purity in spirit and love for the Apple image. At the heart of the campaign, "Think Different" was all about creativity and the new idea would serve a dual purpose of empowering Apple's employees and all the potential customers who would come into the presence of the Apple brand.

The campaign would focus on the "crazy ones." It was about the "crazy ones" who "think different." These individuals were not like the masses. They would not be content with the world as they knew it.

> Here's to the crazy ones. The misfits. The rebels. The troublemakers. The round pegs in the square holes. The ones who see things differently. They're not fond of rules. And they have no respect for the status quo. You can quote them, disagree with them, glorify, or vilify them. About the only thing you can't do is ignore them. Because they change things. They push the human race forward. And while some may see them as the crazy ones, we see genius. Because the people who are crazy enough to think they can change the world are the ones who do.

"Think Different" highlighted many of Steve's heroes. Each of the heroes was an iconic figure. Many of the heroes in the campaign were easily recognizable, including Thomas Edison, John Lennon, Mahatma Gandhi, Bob Dylan, Martin L. King, and Albert Einstein. Those who were not as recognizable were Martha Graham, Ansel

Adams, Richard Fenman, Maria Callas, Amelia Earhart, Frank Lloyd Wright, and James Watson.[59]

Creating the brand for your company will have benefits. Having the right vision and bringing every aspect of your business into alignment with this vision can make a difference over the long term. While it may take years of painstaking effort to truly make a mark on people's perceptions of your product or service, your brand has the potential to bring your firm to the next level of success.

Habit of Knowledge: Learn to Seek Mentors

One way to remember who you are is to remember who your heroes are.
—Steve Jobs

Steve Jobs recognized the value of mentors in business. He quickly realized that he lacked the basic skills to do well in business. It became his personal habit to reach out for personal mentors to get the skills that he lacked in a business. In many ways, Steve would not have progressed as quickly as he did without the help of Nolan Bushnell, John Sculley, Paul Terrell, and Mike Markkula.

Mike Markkula

Mike Markkula was one of the most influential mentors of Steve. More than anyone else, Mike Markkula made it possible for Steve to realize his vision of creating a successful computer company by providing the capital, financing, and management expertise that was sorely needed. Over

THE WINNING HABITS OF STEVE JOBS

the years, Mike provided sage advice when it came to recommending key ideas for the remaking of Apple, sparking the successful return from the brink of insolvency.

In late 1976, Steve Wozniak developed a prototype for a new machine called the Apple II, which could take the company to the next level of having a fully integrated personal computer package. However, the financing of the prototype was out of their reach. Steve estimated that the plastic case alone would require nearly $100,000. Full production of the Apple II would cost about $200,000 or more.[60] To get to this level of investment, they figured they might need to sell the rights of their innovations to a bigger company.

Apple needed help. Steve Jobs's former boss, Nolan Bushnell of Atari, recommended that they call Don Valentine, a founder of Sequoia Capital, an emerging venture capital firm. Although Don Valentine had the ability to finance the venture, he wanted the young company to first gain experience or partner with someone who understood developing a business plan, marketing, and distribution. In his mind, having a good idea was not enough to get established in the computer industry. At Steve's request, Don provided the names of three people he thought could be good partners—one of them was Mike Markkula.

Mike Markkula was a young millionaire. Having worked at Fairchild Semiconductors and Intel Corporation, Mike made millions from his stock options when Intel went public. Even though he was only thirty-three, he was a shrewd man who knew the details of marketing, finance, distribution, and pricing strategies.

He was precise, and Jobs and Wozniak believed he would treat them fairly as a partner.

Markkula also had a vision. He proposed a way ahead that would take personal computers out of the hands of hobbyists and into the market for normal people and families. From Mike Markkula's perspective, the personal computer had the potential to perform household tasks like managing the checkbook and keeping track of the family's favorite recipes. It could be used by everyday workers. Markkula said, "This is the start of an industry. It happens once in a decade."[61]

Mike Markkula was the right mentor at the right time. He provided the necessary financing at a critical time in the young company's path to fame. For the promise of one-third partner equity in the firm, Markkula would provide a line of credit up to $250,000. Steve Jobs, Steve Wozniak, and Mike Markkula would each own 26 percent of the stock. The remainder would be available to attract potential investors. Beyond simply providing financing, Mike Markkula would become a father figure and a mentor. He provided the early training on marketing, distribution, balance sheets, and sales. He even shared his business principles in a one-page document entitled "The Apple Marketing Philosophy." The philosophy emphasized three key points. First, he stressed *empathy*, or the need to connect fundamentally with the needs of the customer. Second, he talked about *focus* and the idea of doing a great job on the top priorities of the company and eliminating distractions. Last, Markkula described the principle of *impute*.[62] He noted that people do judge a book by its cover—and the way in which people form an impression of a company does have an impact on the reputation of the firm. Packaging or pre-sentation of a product, if done in a slipshod manner, would reflect poorly on the company's product and brand.

Steve said, "Mike really took me under his wing...his values were aligned with mine."[63]

Andrew Grove

A second mentor of Steve Jobs was Andrew Grove. An amazing survivor, Andrew Grove was a member of a Jewish family in Budapest, Hungary, during the German occupa-tion and persecution of Jews throughout Europe. When he was eight years old, the German army deported nearly five hundred thousand Jews from Hungary to concentra-tion camps. Through the assistance of friends and taking on false identities, Andrew Grove's family avoided several close calls of being arrested. In 1956, at the age of twenty, he managed to escape Communism during the Hungarian Revolution and fled into neighboring Austria. Andrew continued until he reached the safe harbor of New York City in 1957 and met his future wife, Eva Kastan.

Andrew Grove was a hardworking individual with a deep passion for learning. Through sheer perseverance, he earned a bachelor's degree in chemical engineering at the City College of New York and a doctorate in chemical engineering at the University of California in Berkeley. Shortly after receiving his PhD in 1963, Andrew started as a researcher at Fairchild Semiconductor. In 1967, he became the assistant director of development. In this capacity, Andrew Grove gained unique expertise with the new field of integrated circuits and led the remarkable development of the microcomputer revolution of the 1970s.

In 1968, Robert Noyce and Gordon Moore split away from Fairchild Semiconductor to found Intel. Although Andrew was not considered a founder, he was one of the four who broke away from Fairchild. Andrew provided the important engineering expertise to make Intel successful. He started as Intel's director of engineering and organized the development of its early manufacturing operations. As a persistent innovator, Andrew started with producing dynamic memory chips, called DRAMs, but later he moved toward the more complex skill of manufacturing microprocessors. Andrew was also the key and persuasive negotiator who convinced IBM to use only Intel microprocessors in all of its new personal computers.

Intel Corporation experienced meteoric growth. Within thirty years, Intel's income stream went from $2,672 during its first year of development to more than $20.8 billion by 1997. While the company grew, Andrew Grove became Intel's president in 1979 and CEO in 1987. In 1997, he became Intel's chairman and CEO. Through his dynamic leadership, Intel became one of the world's top manufacturers of microprocessors and the world's seventh largest company with a workforce of sixty-four thousand employees. Andrew Grove was truly a remarkable individual with humble beginnings.

It is little wonder that Steve Jobs called upon Andrew Grove to give him advice when he contemplated taking the position as Apple's CEO. He was a frequent confidant and had a proven track record. Andrew Grove also received accolades by being selected as *Time's* Man of the Year in 1997 and CEO of the Year by *CEO Magazine* in 1997.

Robert Friedland

A third mentor of Steve Jobs was Robert Friedland. Robert was an early associate of Steve when he was learning the skills of sales and entrepreneurship. Interestingly, Robert was the son of immigrant parents who escaped Nazi persecution at the end of World War II. Robert's father, Albert Friedland, survived three years in Auschwitz. His mother, Ilona, served two years of forced labor in a German prison camp. Jobs met Friedland in college. Robert was a senior and student body president at Reed College in Oregon. Robert was the caretaker of an apple farm south of Portland that was owned by his millionaire uncle, Marcel Muller. Steve Jobs and Robert Friedland shared a mutual interest in Eastern spirituality, and the two grew quite close in their beliefs and attitudes. Steve would spend his weekends at the Muller apple orchard, and this association with apples became the inspiration for the company's name.

Robert was given credit for introducing Steve to the reality distortion field. Steve Jobs and Robert Friedland were affected by the practices of Eastern spiritualism and were impressed by the power of the mind to influence people and bend situations to fit their wills. Daniel Kottke, an Apple engineer, observed that many of Jobs's personality traits were learned from Robert Friedland.[64] Through personal example, Friedland taught Jobs how to become an open, mercurial, take-charge, and charismatic leader who could handily influence people and inspire them to do what he wanted.

Later in life, Robert Friedland became a billionaire in the mining industry. Robert was the CEO of Ivanhoe Mines Ltd., based out of Canada, a company he founded in 1994. His leadership led to a successful initial public offering on the Toronto Stock Exchange in 1996. He was the chairman and executive chairman until 2011. Ivanhoe Mines continued to prosper and uncovered a series of gold, silver, and copper deposits in the South Gobi region of Mongolia.

Robert Friedland was one of five business leaders inducted into Canadian Mining Hall of Fame in January 2016. The organizers of this award noted that Robert was "a dynamic, transformative force in the Canadian and international mining industries" and "one of the most recognized mining personalities and achievers in the world."[65] The award citation highlighted his company's building and exploration achievements in the mining industry. Additionally, Robert was selected as the Mining Personality of the Year during the first Asian Mining Awards. Both the Asia Mining Club of Hong Kong and the Mines and Money conference sponsors recognized Friedland's instrumental role in shaping Mongolia's rise as a notable location for mining investment.

Bill Campbell

Often known as the "coach" because of his college football career, Bill Campbell was the vice president for marketing in the early days of Apple. Bill Campbell was born and raised in Homestead, Pennsylvania, which was a short distance from Pittsburgh. A graduate of Columbia University, Bill played college football under Coach Donneli in the late 1950s and early 1960s. He was talented enough to make the All-Ivy team and managed to become the head of the Columbia football team from 1974 to 1979.

His bachelor's degree at Columbia was in economics, and Bill Campbell had a start in an advertisement agency called J. Walter Thompson. Based out of New York City, this advertisement firm became one of the four largest advertisement agencies in the world with more than two hundred offices in ninety countries. He moved to Kodak and was later promoted to manage Kodak's European film business. With these superb business credentials, Bill Campbell was hired by John Sculley to become Apple's vice president. He displayed expertise in software development and was selected to run the Claris software division, which produced such notable programs as MacWrite and MacPaint. With a proven track record of managing software, Bill Campbell served as a corporate director on Apple's board of directors. In time, he became CEO of GO Corporation, specializing in developing a tablet computer operating system with great success. He was CEO of Intuit from 1994 until 1998. Bill Campbell was a great leader and had a commonsense approach to corporate leadership.

Bill fondly recalled Steve's personal invitation to join Apple's board of directors in 1997. Steve and Bill were neighbors in the suburbs of Palo Alto. Steve would often take walks on the weekends and pop into Bill Campbell's home. One day, he simply walked into Bill's yard and sat down beside his pool. With a calm demeanor, Steve said, "I'd like you to join the Apple board."[66]

Without any hesitation, Bill replied, "For sure." The only other time he had such a rush of emotion was when he was asked to be a trustee of Columbia University. The interaction between the two was truly memorable.

During his early days at Apple, Bill Campbell learned how to coach the nation's top technology leaders. As he developed his skills at coaching, Campbell provided sound advice to Jeff Bezos. He worked with Benchmark Capital and Kleiner Perkins. In later years, he coached Evan Williams of Twitter and Eric Schmidt of Google. In all of this, Bill provided his sage advice in an informal setting. You would often find Bill conversing over beer and buffalo wings at the Old Pro sports bar in the heart of Palo Alto. Bill Campbell was an integral part of Apple's advisory board. He spent nearly three decades with Apple after he started as a marketing executive in the 1980s.

Seeking a mentor can accelerate your career. If your mentor is in the same organization, he or she can enhance your reputation within the firm, help you to navigate through the firm's culture, and identify the right personalities to assist your career. Your mentor can assess your strengths and weaknesses and steer you toward the appropriate educational venues and skills to ensure your success. Mentors can provide fresh insights into dealing with challenges and offer alternatives to traditional ways of solving problems. A mentor can be a great motivator to envision the possibilities and inspire you to become even better than you can imagine. Steve made a habit of seeking mentors—and you can also benefit from this proven practice.

Habit of Knowledge: Focus on Location, Location, Location

> Silicon Valley was really the most wonderful place in the world to grow up.
> —Steve Jobs

Few in the wealth-creation business give credit to location. Many assume that the unique skills and talents of Steve Jobs were the key factors in his rapid rise to success. However, we cannot assume that skills alone will create the breaks we need. "Location, location, location" often plays a key, if not critical, role on the path to great success. For some, it may mean relocating to the Big Apple to be immersed in the competitive culture of the trading capital of the US. For those interested in politics, it may mean moving to Washington. Unique expertise, in many cases, can be acquired rapidly by being in the right place and the right time with the right people. In the case of Jobs, location did make a difference. He grew up in the petri dish of computer technology innovation—the burgeoning Silicon Valley of Northern California.

The Bay Area was a premier location for defense investments during the Cold War. The educational institutions of California and the growth of engineering degrees awarded in the Bay Area were distinct attractions for large defense contractors. Stanford University and University of California at Berkeley were two exceptional attractions. The NASA Ames Research Center in Sunnyvale was a fifteen-minute drive from Stanford University. The engineers at NASA invested heavily in computer technologies and cutting-edge technologies in advanced electronics, missiles, voltaics, and nuclear technologies.

Stanford University's dean of engineering, Frederick Terman, invested in the area. Through his vision, he sponsored a seven hundred–acre parcel of land for an industrial park. At this park, graduating students could partner with industry leaders to turn their ideas into world-class products. In the 1970s, thousands of employees were working in the technology sector at Lockheed, Westinghouse, Bell Laboratories, and Hewlett-Packard.

Hewlett-Packard, one of the top electronics companies in the United States, found its origins in Palo Alto. In 1939, Bill Hewlett and David Packard, two electrical engineer graduates from Stanford University started the company in a one-car garage. One of their first products was the precision audio oscillator, the Model 200A, which sold for $54.40. Competitors sold less capable oscillators for more than $200. Over the years, Hewlett-Packard developed exceptional products in personal computers, atomic clocks, sophisticated instrumentation, medical devices, scientific calculators, semiconductor technologies, color printers, and software development. In 2016, Hewlett-Packard boasted total assets of $106.88 billion.

Steve Jobs attributed part of his success to his environment. Like most young kids of his age, Steve became interested in the hobbies of the parents in his neighborhood. One of the cool neighborhood dads was Larry Lange, a Hewlett-Packard engineer who lived seven houses away.

He was a ham radio operator with a garage full of electronic parts. Oftentimes, Larry would drop by with electronic gadgets to play with. One day, he showed Steve a carbon microphone that boosted its sound through a speaker without an electronic amplifier. This innovation amazed Steve and sparked his curiosity in tinkering with electronic devices.

Without a doubt, location played a role in Steve Jobs's success. The habit of seeking the optimum location has benefits. The confluence of skilled experts in the semiconductor and software-development fields occurred in certain locations. Those with the requisite knowledge, skills, and experiences were not available in all parts of the country. Knowing the value of a company's surroundings and the habit of seeking an optimum location can pay dividends for any company.

Habit of Knowledge: Know How to Gain Access and Leverage Other People's Investment

Steve Jobs realized that using other people's money (OPM) was a viable alternative to doing without. In the early days of Apple, Jobs and Wozniak simply did not have the capital to buy even the basic parts for their first order. Despite the early sacrifices of selling Wozniak's scientific calculator for $500 and Jobs's Volkswagen bus, the combined working capital for their business was about $1,300. It was hardly enough to start a business.

Shortly after developing the basic Apple I computer, Jobs and Wozniak planned a presentation for the Homebrew Computer Club. At the large gathering, Jobs emphasized the unique advantages that the Apple computer held over the Altair. He noted that all of the essential components were built into the Apple. He connected with the audience by appealing to their sense of the future of Apple devices and how it would change the industry.

Paul Terrell, a computer business owner who established the Byte Shop in Menlo Park, showed an interest and stayed late to ask more questions about their design. A year later, Terrell had expanded his enterprise to three computer stores and received another demo of the Apple I. This time, Jobs made the sale.

The Byte Shop was a growing business. At the second demo, Paul Terrell seemed less interested in buying printed circuit boards for hobbyists to do their own assembling. Instead, he was willing to buy the Apple I computers that were completely assembled for a cost of $500 apiece. With a total of fifty devices in mind, the total payment for the order would be $25,000, cash on delivery. The one problem that Jobs and Wozniak faced was that they didn't have enough money for the parts for fifty devices.

Buying the complete list of parts for fifty computers would be about $15,000—a large sum of money for the two entrepreneurs. One of their friends, Allen Baum, and his father were willing to loan Jobs $5,000 for the initial order. Jobs approached a bank in Los Altos to arrange a business loan—but it was declined. Another electronic supplier, Haltek Supply, was given the offer of an equal stake in the company for the parts, but the firm turned them down. Atari similarly listened to their offer from Jobs but declined the delivery of parts unless Apple could pay cash in advance. Steve Jobs did not give up. In his drive to succeed, he attempted another technique to leverage other people's money—confirming the Byte Store's credibility and commitment to making a $25,000 purchase order with Apple. Rather than relying on the creditworthiness of two scruffy young entrepreneurs, he would acquire the business credentials of another well-established firm. With Paul Terrell's firm commitment of cash on delivery, Jobs convinced the manager of Cramer Electronics to finance the investment with the delivery of the parts on thirty-day credit.

The opportunity to leverage other people's money can be quite valuable. Jobs was able to refine this habit. At the core of this habit is the skill of communication. Communicating the value of the proposal, the firm commitment of the buyer, and the creditworthiness of the purchaser is a habit that is profitable and repeatable. You can benefit from this habit if you can articulate the profitability prospect to a future investor and be convincing in your projections.

Habit of Knowledge: Know How to Establish Credibility through Other People's Reputations

Steve Jobs wasn't always a household name. In fact, when Jobs started his path toward entrepreneurship, most businessmen looked down upon him. Well, they were not impressed with good reason. Steve was unkempt. He smelled. He didn't shave. His jeans had holes in them. Steve's wardrobe reminded people of a homeless wanderer. Few took him seriously based upon all outward appearances and his lack of business acumen. There was simply not a compelling reason to extend Jobs the credit necessary to start a business as an entrepreneur.

What made up for this difference? What Jobs lacked in experience he made up for through networking with the right people with the right skills and connections. Similar to his phone call to Bill Hewlett, Steve continued to find the right connectors to help his small company's launch. He embarked upon this task with strong resolve and great fervor. Eventually, Steve connected with Regis McKenna, a well-known marketing guru who helped launch Intel as a major player in the semiconductor industry.

Regis McKenna clearly was not impressed with Steve's appearance. He characterized Steve Jobs and Steve Wozniak as slovenly in appearance. In sharp contrast, McKenna was distinguished, polished, and exquisitely dressed. He exuded a magnetic aura. Under normal circumstances, it would be an extreme rarity for McKenna to be seen with such company. Nonetheless, McKenna found a soft spot for Steve due to his piercing intellect and knowledge of computers. Working with Nolan Bushnell, Steve's old boss at Atari, McKenna arranged a meeting with investor Don Valentine.[67]

One connection led to another. Don Valentine was the founder of Sequoia Capital, one of the leading firms that invested in high-tech companies in the Bay Area. Valentine was extremely well-connected and had worked with the founders of Intel prior to their breakup with Fairchild Semiconductors. Don Valentine would prove to be an important connector for the young inventors.

While Valentine didn't personally do business with Jobs, he thought that he owed Regis McKenna a personal favor and helped to introduce the team to Mike Markkula.

Steve Jobs and Steve Wozniak finally hit the gold mine. The introduction to Mike was the only ticket they needed. Markkula had extremely deep pockets. On the advice of Don Valentine, Markkula chose to make the trip to Jobs's garage for a personal visit with the duo. Arriving in a spotless gold Corvette, Mike allowed the team to present their case for the potential of the Apple I computer. Fortunately for Jobs, Markkula had gained in-depth experience with computers while serving as the top sales executive for Intel and earning an advanced degree in electrical engineering. Mike understood the market and knew what was possible. Additionally, Markkula was essentially a computer geek. With these personal inclinations, Markkula recognized the value of the Apple I investment and offered $92,000 to the start-up. He also orchestrated a $250,000 line of credit for them.

Habit of Knowledge: Ladder Up through a Network of Key People

Laddering up is an approach to connect a relatively obscure idea to a broader theme with the potential for a significant return on investment. Within the marketing field, the idea of laddering up is to introduce a nascent company to the latest social media and marketing tools to deliver the best and most effective solutions for the firm. Success in marketing often relies upon creating a substantial and effective digital presence to a wide variety of consumers on a compressed timeline. In the area of networking, it would be to identify key individuals who are connectors to top-notch professionals, allowing you to quickly gain access to someone who was previously unreachable. A ladder-up networking approach would identify intermediate interlocutors who provide access to the best people in your field.

Steve Jobs made networking a habit. In many aspects of his firm, Steve relied upon a network of connected people to provide in-depth understanding, key contacts, and sage advice to resolve problems. A network can provide leverage that might be improbable under normal circumstances. Network connections provided near-instantaneous access to critical information that could provide technical breakthroughs or open doors that previously were closed. As Jobs's reputation grew as an entrepreneur and innovator, his access to a larger network of business professionals grew in leaps and bounds.

The network enabled a technical breakthrough for Apple. During the development of the Apple II computer, Jobs needed a much better power supply for the personal computer. Power supplies in the 1970s put off so much heat that the computer needed an internal fan to keep it cool. Fans were bulky, noisy, and didn't fit into the image that Steve wanted to create with the personal computer. To get after this problem, Steve went to Al Alcorn at Atari to find the right person to solve the problem. Al recommended Rod Holt, a brilliant innovator who was also a tinkerer.

Rod Holt had built his own power supply. In comparison to the standard power supply, which was conventional and linear, Holt created one that operated like an oscillator. Holt's version switched the power on and off rapidly—in some cases thousands of times per second.[68] His invention was revolutionary and helped to make the Apple II computer remarkable in both its circuit board design and its power supply.

A network of supporting people with expertise can be quite valuable. Jobs made it a habit to ladder up through a network of key people. Throughout his career, Steve was always taking the initiative to meet leading professionals in his field and their related suppliers. At times, these professionals were the only ones with the requisite expertise. This networking habit consistently paid great dividends with the developments of the iPod, iPad, and iPhone. You can gain a competitive advantage by developing the habit of laddering up through a network of key people.

Habit of Knowledge: Learn How to Attract A+ Players in Your Field

Motivational speaker Jim Rohn famously claimed that "we are the average of the five people" we spend the most time with. When it comes to relationships, it is not a surprise that—whether it is our choice or not—we are greatly influenced by those individuals who are the closest to us. Also, research conducted at the University of Texas in Austin reveals that we are much more susceptible to our environmental influences than we are aware of.[69]

A+ players are acutely aware of their environment. By definition, A+ players have extremely high standards and value the quality of the people they are subjected to work with. Being compelled to work with B or C players lowers the plane of intellectual discussion, and to some degree, it cheapens the experience of their investment. A+ players value the opportunity to work with other A+ players; that is the first principle of attracting and retaining A+ players in business.

Steve Jobs recognized the value of attracting A+ players. He personally had extremely high standards of performance and only associated with the very best in their fields. Whether it involved finding world-class marketing experts, brand-conscious designers, high-profile entrepreneurs, top-of-the-line engineers, or proven business managers from the commercial sector, Jobs was meticulous at doing his research and finding only the very best that could be attracted to his firm.

Steve Jobs sought only the A+ players in their fields. After the development of the Apple I, Steve realized that the next version would need to be an integrated, complete package with a superior external case, built-in keyboard, and a level of integration that spanned from the power supply to the software products. Instead of targeting the hobbyist consumer, Steve began to set his sights on selling to the thousands of consumers who wanted the computer machine to be fully ready to run. This level of perfection would require a whole new team of partners.

He sought the advice of experienced professionals. Steve had tremendous respect for Nolan Bushnell, the founder of Atari. Bushnell recommended that Steve seek out Don Valentine, a former marketing manager at National Semiconductor and founder of Sequoia Capital. Don Valentine was not impressed with Jobs's appearance or lack of experience with marketing, distribution, and development of business plans. Valentine wisely recommended that Steve approach Mike Markkula for the prerequisite business credentials.

Mike Markkula was a distinguished A+ professional. Having worked at Fairchild and Intel, he had amassed a fortune in millions of stock options when the chip manufacturers went public. Despite being only thirty-three years old, Markkula had already developed extensive experiences in marketing, finance, pricing strategies, and distribution networks. When they first met, Markkula arrived in a gold Corvette convertible. He was decent, respectable, and fair. He had no problem rolling up his sleeves to teach Steve the basics of how to develop a business plan. Not lacking in capital, Markkula offered Jobs a $250,000 guarantee line of credit for a one-third equity partnership.

Habit of Knowledge: Learn How to Monetize Good Ideas that Come from Other Sources

> What a computer is to me is the most remarkable tool that we have ever come up with. It's the equivalent of a bicycle for our minds.
> —Steve Jobs

Steve Wozniak was Jobs's closest friend during his early years at Atari. Wozniak was the tinkering inventor. Jobs, although similarly involved with innovation, was not quite on the same engineering plane as Wozniak. Both were enthralled with the idea of creating a minicomputer that could do basic functions away from the large computer mainframes that were typical in the early 1970s. In many cases, Jobs believed that the minicomputer would be more than an invention; it could literally become an extension and an inseparable part of a person's mind.

The January 1975 issue of *Popular Mechanics* caught the attention of Jobs and Wozniak. On the front cover of this issue lay a picture of the Altair 8800, the first minicomputer kit of its kind. The magazine called it a huge project breakthrough and revealed the potential to rival computer competitors of the time. The article also captured the attention of Paul Allen and his friend Bill Gates, who later launched the development of software for the Altair computer. The Altair kit contained an Intel 8080 microprocessor, 256 bytes of memory, a panel of switches, a case, and an 8-amp power supply. This small package of parts was to be soldered onto an electronic board, and it sparked the interest of tinkerers and electronic hobbyists alike. Although it didn't appear to be much, it was the impetus for a few computer clubs, including the Homebrew Computer Club in the Bay Area.

Steve Wozniak teamed up with Allen Baum to attend a meeting of the Homebrew Computer Club. The first meeting was held on March 5, 1975, in Gordon French's garage in Menlo Park. Wozniak saw potential in the idea of a personally designed microcomputer. He thought it might serve his interests in scientific calculators, pay movies in hotels, television designs, and video games. The club demonstrated the new Altair unit. However, more importantly, Wozniak got to see the specific data sheet on the design of a microprocessor.

The microprocessor or the "chip" changed things. At the time, computer operators had to use remote terminals to do their work. They were connected to distant mainframe computers. These remote terminals were always connected to a large facility with little independence. The beauty of the "chip" was that Wozniak saw the potential to place this device in a terminal and create a stand-alone computer on a desk. It would break with the tradition at the time.

The Homebrew Computer Club meeting gave Wozniak a new idea. He would develop and exploit the idea of a stand-alone computer and come up with a design of his own. Each night after work, he would eat a quick dinner and then return to Hewlett-Packard to moonlight on his new design. He experimented with different micro-processors, including the Motorola 6800, the Intel 8080, and the MOS Technology processor to find the optimum price for the design. Additionally, he would tinker with the best layout for the circuit board in different combinations to perfect the design for his new computer. Later, Wozniak wrote the software code to display his keyboard characters on his own computer screen. He succeeded and showed his work to Jobs.

Steve Wozniak worked on the new device in the spirit of "helping others." He enjoyed the thrill of creating something new; however, he was less concerned about making a profit. Embracing the philosophy of the Homebrew Computer Club, Wozniak believed in sharing and swap-ping freely with fellow experimenters rather than look-ing into the value of a business proposition. He was also extremely shy and unlikely to be the one to market the idea for a commercial audience.

Jobs was enamored with the new design. Jobs recognized and grasped the business potential of the new idea. In short order, Jobs became immersed in the intricate details of creating and enhancing the new minicomputer. He explored the idea of networking the device, developing a disk for memory storage, and buying components such as the random-access memory chips at bargain prices. At each step of the way, Jobs was vitally concerned with component costs and finding the right price point for the commercialization of Wozniak's creation.

Jobs imagined selling electronic circuit boards to the growing entourage of computer hobbyists. He considered hiring an acquaintance at Atari to create fifty circuit boards at a cost of $20 apiece. With that investment of $1,000, Jobs would sell the boards for $50 apiece and net a profit of $700 after costs. Jobs could clearly see market value for Wozniak's designs. With this new idea of selling their new creations, Jobs convinced Steve Wozniak and Ron Wayne to start a new business.

Habit of Knowledge: Become an Uncanny Judge of Character

As with all great leaders, Steve Jobs developed the distinctive ability to read people remarkably well. He was very well-attuned to the emotional quotient in dealing with people. Jobs was a great observer of others and had developed an intuition to know when someone truly knew a subject or was faking it. He recognized people's strengths and vulnerabilities, and he could leverage that uncanny ability to make people feel extremely small or build them up. Steve was a master of persuasion and could make the transition from stroking and flattering to cajoling and intimidating.

One of Steve's strengths was his ability to respect others with the character to stand up to him. That respect hinged on whether the person actually knew what he or she was talking about. Steve had a unique ability to tell if a person was faking it. In some cases, standing up didn't always result in success. Jeff Raskin, the Apple publications manager, eventually failed to keep Steve's respect. To stay in Steve's inner circle, one had to be strong-willed. Boldness—coupled with the strength of true competence—enabled one to gain Jobs's personal respect.

The Macintosh team strove to reward the person who stood up to Jobs. It was an annual award. The first to win this coveted award was Joanna Hoffman, a member of an East European refugee family. A product of the Iron Curtain, Joanna displayed a strong will and a temper. Upon discovery that Steve Jobs had modified her marketing projections to a degree of unreality, she demanded an audience and got Steve to back down on the company's projections. From this interaction, it was clear that Steve was not enamored with surrounding himself with yesmen. As Joanna's credibility grew with Steve, she was provided greater responsibility to take on the bigger projects. The quality of Steve Jobs's circle was an outgrowth of his judgment skills. Being an uncanny judge of character can become a superb habit that leads to true professionalism in every aspect of a company's processes.

Habit of Knowledge: Blend Creativity with Technology

> Creativity is just connecting things. When you ask creative people how they did something, they feel a little guilty because they didn't really do it—they just saw something. It seemed obvious to them after a while.
>
> —Steve Jobs

> Real artists sign their work.
>
> —Steve Jobs

Following the completion of the Macintosh design, Jobs assembled the members of the Macintosh team for a small ceremony. Designers would have a personal stake in the final creation. Jobs said, "Real artists sign their work." With an unremarkable sheet of drafting paper, he insisted that each team member sign his or her name on the paper. He called them out one by one until all forty-six members made their mark on history. Steve Jobs was the last to sign. Champagne was a part of the ceremony, and he toasted the team's accomplishment. These signatures would later be engraved on every single Macintosh computer that was made. Steve had a knack of making every person feel special. It was a memory worth waiting for.

CHAPTER 4

Habits of Execution

Many executives realize that a blockbuster product, a brilliant idea, or a remarkable strategy may get you a place on the map—but it won't keep you there. The only way to remain on the cutting edge of performance is to have solid, effective execution. Any truly successful company will need to prove its worth in execution and deliver on the leadership's intent to remain competitive. Execution is the product of thousands of smaller decisions and practices made every day by the workforce—consistent with the information they have been given and their interests. In the end, the success of a company will be dependent upon the ability of the organization to implement the elements of execution and best practices.

Habit of Execution: Innovate in Execution

> Innovation distinguishes between a leader and a follower.
>
> —Steve Jobs

DR. ROBERT M. TOGUCHI

Sometimes when you innovate, you make mistakes. It is best to admit them quickly and get on with improving your other innovations.

—Steve Jobs

I'm as proud of many of the things we haven't done as the things we have done. Innovation is saying no to a thousand things.

—Steve Jobs

Having a great idea is not enough in life. Without a doubt, ideas without action aren't ideas—they are missed opportunities. How often have we met well-spoken individuals who have a litany of ideas but don't seem to get anything accomplished? Some have undergraduate degrees, some have completed graduate school, and others have an extensive list of proven experiences—but they don't seem to have that mark of distinction.

Innovation is about making things happen. The habit of innovation encompasses the nitty-gritty details of turning good ideas into clear, observable, and measurable outcomes. Innovation requires understanding where we are today in terms of a baseline, projecting a future state when the product or service will be tangibly better, and charting a course that ensures the delivery of the product or service on time. All of this requires hands-on involvement so that nothing is sacrificed and the project is followed through to completion. No one gets credit for being 90 percent finished.

Fixing the iCloud

Innovation is about working out the glitches and fixing problems before they become major issues. Steve Jobs was proactive when it came to enhancing the customer experience. He would not tolerate a blemish on the Apple brand and went to extreme measures to work out the problems for consumers.

In 2001, Steve Jobs had an idea to create a new "digital hub." In this early version, he thought the personal computer would be that digital hub to sync all of the capabilities, including music players, cell phones, tablets, video recorders, and all the other lifestyle devices that a person would need. This vision worked well with Apple's inherent strength, which was creating the end-to-end product that was simple to use for the consumer. This vision became a reality, and Steve Jobs managed to create the experience for the personal computer to become that digital hub.

In 2008, Jobs started to look at the next wave of the digital hub. With his surveillance of the technological possibilities emerging from the labs, Steve believed the personal computer would not remain the hub for future content. Instead, he envisioned that the digital hub would move to the cloud. The beauty of this move was that Apple consumers would be able to access their content from remote servers from anywhere in the world. No longer would they be tied to individual computers. The cloud would be accessible anywhere and anytime.

The problem with the new cloud hub was that it had flaws. For Apple, the glitches had not been worked out. It began with a false step. In the summer of 2008,

Apple offered a product called MobileMe, which was $99 annual subscription service that allowed consumers to access their videos, e-mail, calendars, address books, and files and allow them to sync with any electronic device. It became a nightmare. The technology was too complex, the devices couldn't sync their information, and e-mails were routinely lost between the devices and the receivers. The *Wall Street Journal* reported, "Apple's MobileMe is far too flawed to be reliable."[70]

Steve Jobs possessed the habit of fixing flaws quickly. He was furious at the MobileMe launch problems and wanted answers. Steve summoned the entire MobileMe team into the auditorium at the Apple campus and exploded. "Can anyone tell me what MobileMe is supposed to do? Why doesn't it do that?" The berating continued. "You've tarnished Apple's reputation. You should hate each other for having let each other down. Mossberg, our friend [at the *Wall Street Journal*] is no longer writing good things about us."[71] At the end of his tirade, Jobs fired the lead of the MobileMe team and replaced him on the spot. An eyewitness explained, "Accountability is strictly enforced" at Apple. Jobs believed in accountability, and problems were either fixed or eliminated.

Steve Jobs didn't wait to execute his new fixes. He promptly communicated that he was aware of Clayton Christensen's observation called the innovator's dilemma where the original people who invent a product are "usually the last ones to see past it." Steve recognized that the originators are frequently left behind by ambitious and hungry innovators who leapfrog to the next variation of a technology. Rather than wait for obsolescence, Steve decided to make MobileMe free to consumers. He followed this with the creation of a large server farm in North Carolina to handle any challenges with syncing the new devices.

With these two quick steps, Steve managed to lock in his customers and beat any emerging competition for the cloud. To place the icing on the cake for the iCloud, Steve Jobs brought in the music industry. To beat his competition at Google and Amazon, Steve made exclusive deals with music companies for access on the iCloud. To the amazement of his audience, Steve boasted that "Apple would have eighteen million songs" available on its iCloud servers—something no other competitor could match. Steve guaranteed consumers that Apple would ensure reliable, high-quality music on all of their Apple devices—along with syncing their apps, books, photos, and calendars and that "it would all work together... seamlessly." At the end of this ordeal, Steve proved that he could master execution by outperforming his competition with speed, mastery, and flawless performance.

> Sometimes when you innovate, you make mistakes. It is best to admit them quickly, and get on with improving your other innovations.
>
> —Steve Jobs

Steve Jobs was constantly innovating. In his mind, you will make mistakes as you strive to innovate your way through to a new creation. True innovators are not worried about criticism from others. They create an idea, develop an approach, embrace that approach, and move forward.

True innovators are confident in their abilities and realize that innovation comes about through action. Life is too short to worry about mistakes. Admit them quickly and get on with improving your own innovations.

Innovating in execution means that you own your failures. Embrace every failure. Steve Jobs owned it, learned from it, and took full responsibility for making sure that things would certainly turn out differently the next time. He leveraged failure—in a good way. Great entrepreneurs have failed along the path of innovation. Setbacks are inevitable. However, those who innovate in execution don't miss a beat. They learn from temporary setbacks and persevere through difficulties to get to eventual success.

Habit of Execution: Exemplify Excellence

Be a yardstick of quality. Some people aren't used to an environment where excellence is expected.
—Steve Jobs

Ultimately, it comes down to taste. It comes down to trying to expose yourself to the best things that humans have done and then try to bring those things into what you're doing. Picasso had a saying: good artists copy, great artists steal. And we have always been shameless about stealing great ideas, and I think part of what made the Macintosh great was that the people working on it were musicians

and poets and artists and zoologists and historians who also happened to be the best computer scientists in the world.
—Steve Jobs

Steve attributed the above lesson to his father. In his mind, Apple needed to address the quality of its products based on the right intentions. He believed in providing the best possible product—even though the average consumer would never see the inside components of the Macintosh. Details such as the elegant design of the circuit board—a component that would be hidden inside the plastic box—made a difference to Steve Jobs.

His habit of exemplifying excellence extended to his development of the iPad. Since 2002, Steve was bothered by the technology available to consumers in the form of electronic tablets. At the time, Microsoft engineers were marketing tablet-computer software that would enable input to the computer screen by using a pen or a stylus. It was clumsy and required the use of an additional implement that needed to be carried around. As a consistent habit, Steve was always looking for ways to improve products for consumers. In 2007, Steve Jobs revisited the idea of developing a low-cost netbook computer that was comfortable to use. One of Apple's executive team, Jony Ive, argued that the use of a keyboard attached to a screen would be bulky, clunky, and expensive. Steve agreed. From both of their perspectives, the use of the multitouch technology that was prevalent in the iPhone would be a reasonable approach for creating the ideal computer tablet.

Jobs was a perfectionist when it came to the ideal tablet. With Jony Ive, Steve set about experimenting with various models to determine the exactly right screen size. They tinkered with twenty different models of a tablet with the unique feature of rounded rectangular corners that varied the ratios and sizes of the tablet screens. In this development effort, Steve had the habit of focus. Relentlessly, he realized that the electronic tablet was all about the screen. The screen would be the predominant feature and would drive all improvements. Once the optimum screen was designed, the rest of the tablet would be relatively less important. Jobs knew how to focus and brought this ingrained habit of focus to his products at Apple.

To exemplify excellence, Steve focused on the design of the tablet for comfort. Steve cared deeply about the experience of the consumer, and he was uncomfortable with the current designs. With the help of Jony Ive, Steve identified the problem: the tablet needed to be easily "scooped up" with one hand, and it needed to be able to be "frisked away" on a person's impulse.[72] The designers went to work. The undercarriage of the edge would need to be rounded slightly so that it could by scooped up easily without effort. Also, the ports on the bottom and buttons needed to be tucked neatly under the tablet. All this came to fruition, and a unique Apple patent—D504889—reflected the painstaking efforts by Steve Jobs and Jony Ive to meet the future needs of the consumer.[73]

Even the microprocessor chip needed to be perfected for the iPad. At the time, Intel made the best chips in the world. In many ways, Intel's quality was unmatched, and its manufacturers could boast that the Intel processors were unsurpassed in speed. However, Intel processors were designed to be plugged into a circuit without having to rely on the limitations of battery power and longevity. One of Apple's top engineers, Tony Fadell, argued for a simpler and lower-power chip based on the ARM architecture. Fadell was so confident in his design that he threatened to resign if Steve didn't break with Intel and use the ARM architecture. Steve Jobs's emphasis on amplifying quality and controlling the design extended to the manufacturing of the microprocessor chip. Steve licensed the ARM architecture, and he swung to the extreme of buying a new design company to ensure the quality of the chip. The microprocessor design firm in Palo Alto was called P. A. Semi, and it employed 150 workers. Through Steve's oversight, P. A. Semi developed an original "system on a chip" that was based on the ARM architecture. With this design, Steve paid for the manufacturing to be accomplished in South Korea by Samsung. This habit of excellence extended far beyond the individual features of the iPad and was reflected in Jobs's trademark of an end-to-end design of the product in virtually every aspect of the process. In the end, Steve Jobs controlled the process from start to finish.

Habit of Execution: Routinely Set Long-Term and Short-Term Goals

I think if you do something and it turns out pretty good, then you should go do

119

something else wonderful, not dwell on it
for too long. Just figure out what's next.

—Steve Jobs

Successful people set goals often. Steve Jobs was no
exception. Throughout his life, Steve was consistent in setting long-term and short-term goals. His long-term goals
gave him strategic direction. He also set short-term goals to
keep himself on track. These goals were essential to helping
Steve achieve his vision. His daily goals ensured that he
maximized the use of his time and maintained his ruthless
focus to do the things that mattered most to his business.

After Steve was fired from Apple, he established a
series of goals to get back on track. Many strong-willed
persons would not have fared as well. Others in the same
situation would have become demoralized by the heavy-
handed acts of John Sculley and paralyzed by their hopeless
condition. This was not the case with Steve. Strengthened
by his indomitable will, he deliberately used his habit of
setting long- and short-term goals to reestablish his position as one of the leading entrepreneurs in the country.

His first goal was to find a problem worthy of his prowess and entrepreneurial skills. One month before being let
go by John Sculley in August 1985, Steve Jobs contacted
Paul Berg, a Stanford biochemist, to get an update on
recombinant DNA and gene-splicing. Steve asked Paul
about the possibilities of replicating experiment results on
a computer instead of conducting live experiments in a
lab. Paul Berg responded that computers with that kind of
power were too expensive for university labs. Berg recalled
that Steve became extremely excited about the prospects

based on their conversation.[74] He planned to start a new company to develop a computer with the capacity to meet the needs of the academic community. Steve achieved his goal of finding a worthy problem for a new company.

Steve's second goal was to identify key individuals with the appropriate expertise to help him form a new computer company. Loyal Apple workers would be needed for their specialized skills in meeting the computing demands of the academic community. Rich Page, the chief engineer for the Apple's Big Mac version of the Macintosh for academic researchers, approached Steve with a query about job prospects. Steve encouraged his move. Next, Steve contacted Bud Tribble, the Macintosh's original software developer, and hinted at the idea of building a company that would produce a more powerful and personal workstation. Bud Tribble agreed to support the move and recruited controller Susan Barnes and engineer George Crow. Jobs approached and gained a commitment from Daniel Lewin, the marketer at Apple who had organized a consortium of universities to buy Macintosh computers. Steve was a fast mover, and he initiated his comeback with short, concise goals.

Steve's third goal was to set conditions to establish the brand of his new company. He began by establishing the company's name: NeXT. Steve courted and hired the corporate dean of logos, Paul Rand, to design a world-class logo for this emerging company. With brilliance and conciseness, Rand offered Steve only one option for the design: a black cube tilted at a twenty-eight-degree angle. "Tipped with a jaunty angle, it brim[med] with the informality, friendliness, and spontaneity of a Christmas seal and the

DR. ROBERT M. TOGUCHI

authority of a rubber stamp."[75] He also recast the name to NeXT to emphasize the little *e* such as in e=mc^2. Steve listened to Rand's presentation of the logo and hugged him. The price tag for the world-class logo was $100,000.

The fourth goal was to solicit prominent investors who could finance the large project and bring name recognition and credibility to buttress NeXt's reputation. In 1986, Steve advertised to venture capital firms an offering of a 10 percent stake in his company for $3 million. That placed a valuation for NeXT at $30 million. Fortunately for Steve, Ross Perot, the wealthy Texan who had established Electronic Data Systems (EDS), happened to watch *The Entrepreneurs* on PBS in November 1986. The PBS documentary highlighted the exploits of Steve Jobs and the founding of NeXT. Ross Perot called the next day and said, "If you ever need an investor, call me."[76] Steve waited a week, followed up, and secured his key investor who would make everything work.

Setting goals is an important habit. Compelling goals set the course for personal development and success. Goals provide structure to a personal vision and identify the necessary steps to get you to the outcome. They are empowering and give renewed energy and life to your actions. Goals should be measurable and provide timely and important feedback on your progress toward achieving your vision. Goals should be aligned with your values. This alignment will ensure consistency and help prioritize what is most important to your life.

Habit of Execution: Impute Quality into Your Brand

> When you're a carpenter making a beautiful chest of drawers, you're not going to use a piece of plywood on the back, even though it faces the wall and nobody will see it. You'll know it's there, so you're going to use a beautiful piece of wood on the back. For you to sleep well at night, the aesthetic, the quality, has to be carried all the way through.
>
> —Steve Jobs

Steve Jobs learned early in his career the value of imputing quality into the brand. Customers have become extremely keen observers of detail in their products. Minute details that may not seem obvious to designers have become quietly inescapable to discerning consumers who purposefully search for the discriminating features between brands. To many consumers, quality has become the quintessential differential that determines what they buy.

Steve Jobs recognized the criticality of making a first impression on the consumers of his Apple products. The creation of the Apple package was a paramount importance to Steve. Something as simple as the look and feel of the box in which an Apple product was featured was a significant design feature. Clean, simple, powerful design lines sent a powerful message to the consumer that Apple was unlike any other product they had purchased. It imputed excellence from the very beginning of the consumer experience.

DR. ROBERT M. TOGUCHI

Color and shading served a vital part of the experience. The selection of the color white was a conscious choice of the Apple team to connote elegance, simplicity, and purity. Steve's initial instincts were against white.[77] However, Jony Ive loved white products and had been building white plastic models since he was in school. Jony Ive claimed that he started making Apple products white in reaction to the wild color phase of the iMac. Apple made the iBook and the iPod in white. Steve continued to use white in his newer products. The Apple brand was very important to Steve Jobs. To create the ideal experience, Steve began to toy with the idea of enhancing the customer experience through the creation of Apple stores. In late 1999, he began the interview process of finding the top candidate to develop a number of Apple retail stores. In his quest, he uncovered Ron Johnson, the merchandising vice president for Target and a distinct innovator for the launching of unique products.

Jobs viewed the Apple store as part of the Apple experience. His products were slightly more expensive than generic computer brands such as Dell and Compaq. In his mind, those computers were made for the masses and could not compare with the distinctive quality of an iMac. The look and feel of the Apple store would contribute to the customers' impressions of what the Apple brand was all about.

Steve Jobs's adviser, Ron Johnson, conveyed the importance of the in-store experience. He asked, "Is Apple as big of a brand as the Gap?"[78] Jobs believed that Apple's brand was much bigger than the Gap, and thus, the store experience must surpass it. Jobs noted that a great company must impute its brand and communicate its importance through the entire experience from "packaging to marketing." Johnson said, "The store will become the most powerful expression of the brand."[79] Johnson distinctly remembered his first experience in the majestic, wood-inlaid-paneled, artistic mansion of a Ralph Lauren store in Manhattan. Every time he purchased a Polo shirt, Johnson romantically recalled the Ralph Lauren mansion experience, which was a distinct "expression of the Lauren ideals." Steve Job agreed. The brand is conveyed through the store experience.

In the end, Steve Jobs designed the ideal Apple store. The first Apple store opened at Tyson's Corner, Virginia, in 2001 with a splash. While Gateway stores averaged 250 visitors per week, Apple stores averaged 5,400 visitors in 2004. Its revenue broke retail store records with an amazing $1.2 billion in revenue in one year. The Manhattan Fifth Avenue version of the Apple store opened its doors in 2006. Contrary to the skeptics, the Manhattan store took in more income "per square foot than any other store in the world."[80] The successful trend with the Apple retail experience continued. In 2011, a short decade after the first store opened, Apple had a total of 326 stores. Each store averaged an annual income of $34 million; total net sales in 2010 were $9.8 billion.[81]

Quality is important to any brand. In retrospect, the impression created by the Apple store experience had a lasting effect on customer perceptions and sales. Jobs spared no expense in managing the details of the Apple store and reaped the benefits of his investment. First impressions make lasting impressions—and your attention to quality will find its expression in your bottom line.

DR. ROBERT M. TOGUCHI

Habit of Execution: Impute Being in Control: Learn to Open with a Splash

What is Apple, after all? Apple is about people who think "outside the box," people who want to use computers to help them change the world, to help them create things that make a difference, and not just to get a job done.

—Steve Jobs

Steve Jobs mastered the art of the opening. This quality was undeniable. It followed Jobs in every aspect of his career. Why be boring? What does one lose if you choose to open with a splash? Does your personal brand suffer or gain tremendously from a little pizzazz? Jobs's personal style emphasized the latter with amazing results.

The 1984 Macintosh ad for Super Bowl XVIII serves as a powerful example. In the spring of 1983, Jobs wanted a revolutionary opening. He literally wanted "something that will stop people in their tracks" and boldly stated, "I want a thunderclap."[82] However, there is a big difference between wanting to deliver a thunderclap and being able to deliver on a desire. Jobs had the unique ability to deliver.

He started by hiring the best. For this huge task, Steve picked the Chiat/Day advertising agency of Los Angeles. This company had an edgy feel, and its office was located in Venice Beach. Lee Clow, the creative director, looked like a disheveled beach bum. He had wild hair, an overly bushy beard, and a weird smile that went along with the LA crowd. However, under all of this wildness, Lee Clow had a unique, savvy way about him that would bond his relationship with Steve Jobs for decades.

Lee Clow played off the idea of the George Orwell novel tagline: "Why 1984 won't be like *1984*?"[83] The storyboard for the sixty-two second ad seemed like a screenshot from a twenty-first-century science fiction movie. With a hazy gray aura, it would feature an almost Olympian-fit, young woman rebel clearly outrunning the thought police with a huge sledgehammer. With sweaty determination, she would hurl this Thor-like sledgehammer into a huge screen depicting a mind-controlling picture of Big Brother. Big Brother at the time would be IBM being challenged by the Apple underdog. The Macintosh would be the cool warrior that would defeat the clutches of the evil IBM corporate plan for world domination.

Lee Clow's vision for the ad fit Steve Jobs's personality. Steve viewed himself as a rebel. His ragged team of rugged individualism that developed the Macintosh were, in some fashion, fighting the corporate image of the IBM competition. The Mac team was more akin to pirates and hackers than the stiff and stuffy image of the IBM culture. Steve clearly saw himself as the embodiment of the competing counterculture.

Jobs hired Ridley Scott, the director of *Blade Runner*, which had turned out to be a blockbuster hit with a science fiction setting and cyber-edginess for the 1980s. Ridley Scott would hire a number of real London "skinheads" to replicate the mindless masses that would be listening to the Big Brother on the large screen. The female heroine was a muscular discus thrower with distinctive features. Recreating the gray, inner-city aura of *Blade Runner*, the heroine would race and then launch the sledgehammer into the screen as Big Brother shouted, "We shall prevail!" After a loud explosion, flashing lights, and smoke, the skinheads would watch in horror as the background voice announced, "On January 24, Apple Computer will introduce Macintosh. And you'll see why 1984 won't be like '1984.'"[84]

The ad was an overnight sensation. All three national networks—CBS, NBC, and ABC—raved about the advertisement as being the top selection for Super Bowl fans. Fifty local television stations chimed in. The piece had a viral sensation as millions viewed and buzzed about the ad. *Advertising Age* and *TV Guide* portrayed it as the greatest ad of all time.

Habit of Execution: Master the Ability to Zoom Out and Zoom In

> A lot of [what it means to be smart] is the ability to zoom out, like you're in a city and you could look at the whole thing from the 80th floor down at the city. And while other people are trying to figure out how to get from point A to point B reading these stupid little maps, you could just see it in front of you. You can see the whole thing.[85]
>
> —Steve Jobs

Steve Jobs was a master at observing others in his work environment. Of note, he perceived that so-called "smart" people frequently make connections that seem simple to themselves but extremely perplexing to others around them. Smart people appear to do this routinely. According to Steve, the skill that they have mastered is the ability to "zoom out" and to "zoom back in" to gain a wider and more comprehensive view of the big picture.

How exactly do you gain the ability to "zoom out" and to "zoom in?" According to Steve Jobs, varied experiences throughout one's career is the key. At times, you can be the most knowledgeable person in the room, based on your previous experiences. You don't necessarily have to be a world-class or global expert in a particular field; you must merely strive to know significantly more than the average leader in your organization to shine as a strategic leader. Undoubtedly, there will be many opportunities throughout one's career to acquire unique experiences. Experiences can come in the form of internships, sabbaticals, summer trips, in-depth documentaries, and just spending thoughtful time with others who have unique experiences.

You have to not have the same bag of experiences as everyone else does, or else you're gonna make the same connections and you won't be innovative.... You might want to think about going to Paris and being a poet for a few years. Or you might want to go to a third-world country—I'd highly advise that.[86]

The inquisitive mind, which we mentioned in the early section of this book, is another key. Having an inquisitive mind ensures that you are generally open to new experiences and listening to the experiences of others who may

DR. ROBERT M. TOGUCHI

appear to be different in background, disciplines, skill sets, markets, and environments. Hence, the link to diversity is important to understanding the dynamics of open experiences as it relates to the bottom line. Being open to new experiences explains why some can routinely "zoom out" to a realm of thinking that is completely foreign to most leaders in the room.

Habit of Execution: Persuasive Communications

Steve Jobs practiced the art of effective and persuasive speaking. Like many charismatic leaders, Steve learned how to employ different communication strategies that adapted to varying situations and audiences.[87] At the same time, he varied his strategy. Steve managed to deliver a constant theme or message to his audiences.[88] Steve practiced great sophistication by analyzing the amount of credibility or ethos he held with the recipients of his communication.

Through the lens of Aristotle's classic tools of persuasion, Dr. Loizos Heracleous, a professor at the Warwick Business School of Rhode Island, used the framework of ethos, pathos, and logos to study how Steve Jobs selected different strategies to deliver his message. Ethos represented the amount of credibility that Steve had with his audience. Pathos indicated an appeal to the emotions of his audience through the use of figurative language, metaphors, and personal stories to relate to those listening to his speech. Logos stood for his use of facts, statistics, and logical arguments to convince the audience of his point of view.

By studying Steve Jobs's speeches, Dr. Heracleous discovered a pattern of behavior. He found that Steve had a driving factor in his behavior (his perceived ethos). When Steve thought he had a low ethos or low credibility with his audience, he resorted to a pathos approach of appealing to the emotions of his audience through figurative speech, personal stories, and metaphors to convince them of his genuineness. On the other hand, when Steve perceived that he had a high ethos or high credibility with his audience, he changed his rhetoric toward logos—a factual approach to convincing audiences of his position. In all of this, Steve delivered a message that remained consistent through his personal engagements.

Dr. Heracleous observed that charisma is not an unusual magical quality that cannot be understood. He determined that one can learn the art of charismatic communication by studying practitioners such as Steve Jobs. He noted that charisma is a "consequence of the relationships among leader, audience, and context."[89]

Steve Jobs practiced this dynamic relationship of varying his strategies according to the context of his audience and his position as a leader. His performance was a key factor in his remarkable success as a business leader. To a significant degree, your ability to communicate persuasively will have an impact on your overall success.

Habit of Execution: Master the Ability to Critique

Steve Jobs was a master at critiquing a product, innovation, or idea. This created the overall effect of motivating employees to do their absolute best in the aftermath of the critique. Steve did not have a middle ground when it came to critiquing ideas. Walter claimed a "key aspect of

Jobs's worldview was his binary way of categorizing things. People were either 'enlightened' or 'an asshole.' Their work was either 'the best' or 'totally shitty.'"[90]

Bill Atkinson became a close observer of the good side of the dichotomies. From Bill's perspective, there was a "great polarity" between "gods" and "shitheads." If Steve categorized you as a "god," you essentially could do no wrong and remained on a type of pedestal. Once in that position of "doing no wrong," team members would strive to stay in Steve's good graces since the perceived benefits were immense. With this positive treatment, Steve had the ability to inspire team members to "share his passion" and accomplish the "seemingly impossible."[91] Once there, members were constantly afraid of being knocked off their pedestals. The bottom line is that they worked even harder to maintain their positions.

Steve labeled certain workers "shitheads." In many cases, those workers in the negative category were brilliant engineers. They worked extremely hard to impress Steve Jobs and often felt that "there was no way they could get appreciated and rise above their status."[92] An outcome of the negative critique was that the workforce did nearly everything possible to impress Steve in a favorable way. Even his negative critiques resulted in a keen desire and motivation to do better.

The categories could change unpredictably. Steve was known to reverse his position overnight and label a person's work as totally awful the next day. Bud Tribble noted that Steve resembled a high-voltage alternating current. Nobody would know when the high voltage would turn from praise to an absolutely scalding critique.

Steve Jobs became a master at manipulating his unfiltered behavior. According to Andy Hertzfeld, he was emotionally attuned to his team members and developed an uncanny ability to read people. Steve gained a certain mastery of knowing each team member's psychological strengths and vulnerabilities. At times, he demonstrated an ability to stun a victim with a deliberate, well-timed emotional snap. Steve developed unique skills at influencing, stroking, intimidating, and pandering to his team members. While such behavior may not work for everyone, developing skills to understand individual behaviors and staying emotionally connected can have a powerful effect.

Habit of Execution: Amplify Simplicity

That's been one of my mantras—focus and simplicity. Simple can be harder than complex; you have to work hard to get your thinking clean to make it simple.

—Steve Jobs

Ron Wayne believed Atari's leadership climate influenced Steve Jobs's approach to the workplace. In his early career, Nolan Bushnell was the CEO for Atari. The philosophy at the time was to create products that exemplified simplicity. Atari's first game, *Star Trek*, reflected this philosophy. It had no operator manual. It had no complicated rules. Its approach was simple: insert quarter, avoid Klingons, stay alive. Steve embraced simplicity in his design, in his communications, and in his portrayal of a new invention.

The iPhone was a great example of simplicity at work. To Steve Jobs, making a product very easy to use was a key to simplicity. Viewing the phone from a customer's point of view, Steve Jobs thrived on making the experience simple and elegant. To get to the heart of simplicity, Steve thought deeply about all the features of a smartphone.

With the iPhone, Jobs looked at the user interface and searched for ways to revolutionize the experience. At the time, the hot competitors were the BlackBerry, the Palm Treo, Nokia, and Motorola phones. What did these smartphones have in common? They had a keyboard with little plastic buttons and were complex in every way possible. The buttons got smaller and smaller, and you practically needed a magnifier to get at each one of them. Steve threw all of the nefarious keyboards out and created a large screen made of gorilla glass. In one move of unique engineering design excellence, Steve revolutionized the smartphone industry. The end result was that Steve's bold decision changed the face of the cell phone forever, and his innovation amplified Apple's brand of simplicity and elegance. For Steve Jobs, this was a habit.

Habit of Execution: Value the Importance of Time

> My favorite things in life don't cost any money. It's really clear that the most precious resource we all have is time.
> —Steve Jobs

Time is a critical component of the entrepreneur experience. Competition in a lucrative industry is extremely vigorous and intense. Cutting-edge companies collect the latest and most important details of other companies. Oftentimes, the first to market allows one company to dominate the market and create an impression of product superiority.

Deadlines are key to any competitive industry. Time is money. Cutting the time to ship a product reduces the overhead costs associated with a project. Cutting the time to market creates a distinctive advantage over the competition. Cutting the time to supply parts reveals the attributes of a successful company that is organized, efficient, and highly effective in delivering quality to consumers.

In some cases, deadlines can be detrimental. In some cases, deadlines provide general guidelines or parameters that can slow a project. For example, it may take two weeks to resolve a certain software problem. Members of the workforce may naturally meter their performance to take the entire two weeks—even though advice from the right professionals might have cut the time to one week. Steve was not like that. Exceptional leaders impose their will on time and frequently surpass expectations by delivering products early and to higher standards.

Steve Jobs was a master of taking advantage of time. He quickly determined the amount of time needed to develop a product and set goals far short of that timeline. He knew instinctively how to motivate his workforce and manage that compressed timeline. Few could have done what Jobs did in maximizing the effectiveness of his developmental teams at Apple.

Other entrepreneurs recognize the importance of time in being successful. Mark Cuban noted that time was his number 1 asset in business. Mark claimed, "How wisely you use your time will have far more impact on your life and success than any amount of money."[93]

When Mark Cuban was twenty-five, he started a software-solution distributor called MicroSolutions. After achieving a small amount of success, the company's secretary stole $83,000 of the company's $85,000. Mark bounced back. He claims that his judicious use of precious time in studying PC code writing and software gave him the essential edge over his competitors. Within a few years, Mark Cuban was able to sell MicroSolutions to H&R Block for $6 million.

Habit of Execution: Be a Team Builder

> My model for business is The Beatles. They were four guys who kept each other's kind of negative tendencies in check. They balanced each other and the total was greater than the sum of the parts. That's how I see business: great things in business are never done by one person, they're done by a team of people.
> —Steve Jobs

Jobs believed in people. He was a master of understanding people—their motivations, their creativity, their inspiration, and their aspirations. All great businessmen are able to build a team, including John D. Rockefeller,

Thomas Edison, and Henry Ford. These great men started with an idea and sought the collective wisdom of a team to realize their dreams.

One of the strongest teams Jobs assembled was the team that created the Macintosh. Repeatedly, Steve referred to this experience as one of the defining moments in his life. The Macintosh team was a world-class team in which each member was handpicked to be a part of this dream team. Jobs took great care in selecting ambitious engineers with extraordinary talent and deep passion for the project he was working on. He would often set up a test by covering a prototype of the Macintosh with a small cloth and unveiling the revolutionary product only to closely watch the reaction of the new prospect. If the candidate expressed the "wow" factor and went straight to playing, pointing, and clicking with the mouse...Steve often hired them on the spot.[94]

Vision was critical. Steve Jobs was a master of making a team believe in a purpose that was bigger than anyone could achieve on their own. The vision of creating an affordable computer for the masses with a graphic user interface instead of a text interface compelled the team to think of something larger and bigger than themselves.

Steve created a unique environment for his team. Able to separate his team from distractions, Steve picked a two-story building several blocks away from Apple corporate headquarters. The "Texaco Towers," named after their adjacent spot to a Texaco gas station, embodied a setting more akin to a convention for a geek squad and its toys.

True leaders know how to build the team. Steve Jobs was no exception. Being a leader in many cases was purely intuitive. Steve possessed quite a few talents that were early harbingers of truly great leaders. Despite his rough edges, Steve exuded charisma, was extremely insightful and innovative, and harbored the deep passion to drive his team to excellence in everything they undertook.

Habit of Execution: Make Quality a Part of Everyday Life

We think the Mac will sell zillions, but we didn't build the Mac for anybody else. We built it for ourselves. We were the group of people who were going to judge whether it was great or not. We weren't going to go out and do market research. We just wanted to build the best thing we could build.[95]

—Steve Jobs

For Steve, the motivation for why he created a product was important. Money was not his primary motivation for creating the Mac. There was an intrinsic value associated with the Mac. It was more than a way to amass millions of dollars. From the very beginning, it was about creating a product he would value. The Mac was the best thing that Steve's team could build.

Quality is much better than quantity. One home run is much better than two doubles.

—Steve Jobs

Quality was certainly a defining habit of Steve Jobs. It was a consistent theme that ran throughout his career at Apple, NeXT, and Pixar. In fact, quality was a genuine obsession that followed Steve in all his endeavors. Merely meeting the design specifications for a product was not enough to Steve. He surpassed normal supervisor standards to ensure that the products went beyond the consumer's expectations.

Steve Jobs learned about quality from his father. Paul Jobs ensured that his son took pride in his craftsmanship. When Paul Jobs worked on interior cabinets for homes, he guaranteed that the external quality of the cabinet reflected the best materials and workmanship and made sure that the back of the cabinets upheld the same quality standards. Paul Jobs taught Steve to perfect the parts of the cabinet that people couldn't see. This lesson remained with Steve for the rest of his life. This habit reflected the quality of Apple products.

Steve brought the same degree of quality scrutiny to the interior of the Macintosh. Steve critiqued the printed circuit board that encased the integrated chips and electronic components that made up the Macintosh. No consumer would get to see the inside the Macintosh, but Steve made sure that the aesthetics were brought to a high standard. When one of the Apple engineers stated, "Nobody is going to see the PC board," Steve replied, "I want it to be as beautiful as possible, even if it's inside the box. A great carpenter isn't going to use lousy wood for the back of a cabinet, even though nobody's going to see it."[96]

CHAPTER 5

Practical Steps for Applying Winning Habits

S teve Jobs developed and refined habits that made him successful. His daily routine provided clear evidence of a purposeful design of his time to maximize his effectiveness as a CEO and innovator. Steve studied and learned from business entrepreneurs he chose to associate with. With the right role models, Steve was able to remake himself into an entrepreneur who excelled in all of his undertakings.

Knowing the habits of Steve Jobs is not enough to replicate his success. Ultimately, to make a difference, today's entrepreneur must learn significant ways to apply and instill selected habits into his or her daily life. Without adapting and changing one's habits, an entrepreneur might be a good student but not be capable of experiencing the relative success in the workforce or marketplace. To advance this thought, we will discuss potential ways in which a person can create successful daily habits. The list below includes the first steps in establishing the practice of creating new habits.

Foster an Inquisitive Mind

Not everyone is born with a fervent desire to read or possesses the innate spark of intellectual curiosity. In many cases, the habit of learning can be inspired and nurtured within an individual. Knowing that an inquisitive mind can lead to numerous benefits, daily reading can be established through practice. Through habit stacking, one can develop the habit of reading in the evening prior to sleep. The daily habit of brushing one's teeth can be coupled with the determination to read thirty minutes prior to bedtime. With practice, a daily routine can easily become a habit that is lasting and enduring. Other ways to learn could include listening to favorite books during your daily commute. That time can provide an opportunity for hours of learning each day.

Be a Committed Problem Solver

Steve Jobs relished the opportunity to solve problems. Instead of relying upon others, he took an active role in contemplating and applying solutions to resolve technical problems. Entrepreneurs can develop this habit by developing a step-by-step routine. The following example is provided for illustrative purposes.

First, establish the desire to create the new product and see it to completion. Next, envision the end state or outcome that would make the product distinctly better than the competition. Third, take an active role in identifying the specific problems or challenges that need to be resolved. Fourth, use your personal or extended network to find the best practitioners with the expertise to solve the problem.

Leverage their expertise or employ their services to find a technical solution. Last, orchestrate the completion of the end-to-end design with singular focus to bring about the best possible product or service. These steps are not dissimilar to those used by Steve Jobs. Through a committed use of a step-by-step routine, an entrepreneur can develop ingrained habits for solving problems.

Create the Vision

In any worthwhile endeavor, creating the vision has been a key habit to success. Steve Jobs was a master at making his team believe in a higher purpose that was bigger than anyone could possibly achieve alone. With the Macintosh, Steve's vision of creating an affordable computer for the masses with a graphic user interface instead of a text interface compelled the team to think of something larger and bigger than themselves.

Like Steve Jobs, each person has the potential and the ability to create the vision. You can create a winning vision by contemplating the potential future for your business or organization. Whether it is articulating the next-generation capabilities for man-machine interfaces, augmented reality, social-media analytics, biometrics, or cloud computing, you can become an influential leader who can instill a deep desire among your peers and workforce to create the best future for your organization.

Routinely Set Long- and Short-Term Goals

Steve Jobs was consistent in establishing goals. You can do the same. Through habit stacking, you can set daily goals by ensuring that you write down five to eight key tasks to accomplish that day before you have your first cup of coffee. By adding this step, you can structure your work habits for the next twenty-four hours.

On some days, you may not accomplish all the tasks. Nonetheless, by consistently setting daily habits, you will begin to see marked improvement in your daily performance. As your effectiveness in accomplishing tasks improves, you can slowly add more tasks to your daily lists. Similarly, you can learn to establish short-term goals for the month and quarter and longer-term goals for the year. The decision to establish goals routinely will contribute tangibly to your overall success.

Guard Your Heart—Follow Your Passion

Steve Jobs embraced the daily habit of following his passion. For Jobs, it wasn't about the money. He knew how to focus his efforts to follow what was near and dear to his heart. He realized that passion would enable him to invest the necessary time and energy to become a success in the career field of his choice. Passion would carry him through the difficult times and inspire him to continue the journey when others had given up. Passion was necessary for career success.

You also can follow your passion in your career. The first step you can take is finding your passion. A way to identify your passion is to observe what you do with your spare time. Friday evenings, Saturday afternoons, and Sunday evenings provide opportunities for people to explore their passions. What activities do you gravitate toward in those free moments during the week? What do you find interesting in the subjects you read? What natural skills and abilities provide you an idea of what you enjoy? In your areas of passion, it feels like play instead of work.

Steve Jobs had to choose between following his passion and making money. In several cases, Steve lost money to do what he believed was the right thing to do. His return to Apple was less about making money and more about doing the right thing and satisfying his inner passion. You also can follow your inner passion by making critical decisions about your business and your career. You will always do much better in areas where you feel great passion.

Innovate by Connecting the Dots

Steve Jobs mastered the habit of innovation. He recognized that connecting the dots was more than identifying unique relationships; it was part of a chain of connections. Steve was able to find the new dots through strategic partnerships with those who had specialized expertise in a field in which he needed information. Without finding the new dots, his thinking—and that of Apple—would be limited to in-house expertise, and he would not be able to make the grand breakthroughs that were essential in his field.

Finding a new dot with the Corning Corporation led to the breakthrough of Google Glass, which was essential to the iPhone's success. Steve catalogued the dots so he could quickly and easily access the dots to help him with solving a problem. Steve found a way to network the dots based on the innovative approach that he took to solve a problem. Each approach used a different combination of dots that was unique to his approach. After connecting the dots, Steve was able to forecast the dots to know where the trend was taking his company, the competition, and the global market. In many ways, forecasting the dots can be much more valuable than just connecting the dots.

Steve Jobs frequently looked to the intersection of two or more separate fields or disciplines to identify new capabilities that synergy provides. You can benefit from this habit. When you schedule a brainstorming session to determine alternative ways to accomplishing an objective, be sure to invite key individuals from other disciplines. If the best employee in your office is an engineer, try inviting artists or marketing, design, media, or sales professionals who will likely bring different mind-sets and different problem-solving approaches to the same challenge. Your meetings will become more productive when you recognize the valuable, innovative habit of connecting the dots.

Become a Purveyor of Big Ideas

This habit involves gaining exposure to those who conceive of the big ideas. Steve Jobs made it a recurring habit to look for big ideas among innovators. Even at an early age, he and Steve Wozniak searched the local Homebrew Computer Club meetings in Menlo Park to hear from the latest innovators in circuit boards and create a hobbyist version of a computer. Steve loved to read magazines such as *Popular Electronics* and the *Whole Earth Catalog* to look for innovators.

With recommendations from Jeff Raskin and Bill Atkinson, Steve sought the big ideas by visiting the Xerox Palo Alto Research Center (PARC) facility where he was exposed to the graphic user interface (GUI) and ideas for a "mouse." Recognizing the early stages of an industry break-through, Steve seized upon the potential and brought these ideas into the Macintosh. The revolutionary innovations were an outgrowth of linking disparate pieces of informa-tion that Steve had acquired through exposure. It was a habit. Entrepreneurs can nurture a habit of exploring big ideas by designating time each day to read innovative pub-lications and find like-minded innovators.

Ladder-Up Networking of Key Partners

Having a network can serve as a multiplier effect to speed up accomplishments, identify new possibil-ities, and provide sound advice for a growing business. Knowledge is not enough. To foster this habit, an entre-preneur must set aside time each day to plan and engage in outreach to build a network. Through the practice of habit stacking, one can designate a specific time each day to make targeted phone calls to widen the circle of key partners. Through personal contacts, one can begin to identify professionals who could contribute to your busi-ness. Volunteer organizations, charities, or professional groups such as Business Networking International, Young Entrepreneurs Council, Toastmasters International, the

Lions Club, alumni associations, and country clubs are opportunities for networking and contacts.

Professional conferences for like-minded individuals may expose entrepreneurs to leaders in the field. Those who take the initiative to create their own personal networks of professionals create opportunities.

Seek Mentors

Mentors are the fastest way to gain expertise in any field. Steve Jobs was not afraid to seek and embrace mentors in computer and electronics technology. Mike Markkula, Bill Campbell, Robert Friedland, Andrew Grove, Bill Gates, and Larry Ellison were just a few of the people from whom Steve sought advice. Start the journey today. Leverage the contacts in your personal network, seek sponsors, and acquire mentors in your field.

Uncommon Focus

Steve Jobs demonstrated a strong habit of providing uncommon focus to his projects. For some, the habit of focus may take determination and a strong will. Nonetheless, through regular practice, one can master the daily habit of focus in the workplace. As Steve demonstrated, it takes ruthless focus to eliminate distractors from performance and do only those things that bring entrepreneurial success. Simple steps can be taken to eliminate distractions.

Place your office farthest from the entrance so that it is harder for visitors to distract you. Designate a regular time for phone calls, a set time for answering e-mails, and a specific time for staff meetings. Routinize all recurring tasks. Stop doing tasks that are not directly tied to your purpose. Delegate tasks that can be done by others. If possible, give administrative tasks—advertising, mailing letters, scheduling rooms, setting up teleconferences, and printing schedules—to others. By studying and applying the habits of focus of Steve, people can gain control of their daily schedules and begin to increase personal effectiveness. Get started by taking small steps that will lead to significant advances in focus.

Value the Importance of Time

Steve Jobs was the master at taking advantage of time. He quickly realized the amount of time needed to develop a product and set goals far short of that timeline. He knew instinctively how to motivate his workforce and managed that compressed timeline relentlessly. Few could have done what Jobs did in maximizing the effectiveness of his developmental teams.

You can make the most of your time. Set life priorities, develop clear goals, create actionable checklists, and eliminate distractions to maximize the use of time. Habits associated with time management are some of the best indicators of overall success. Establishing priorities exposes the unnecessary tasks in life. In the end, time is a precious and limited commodity. Aligning your time with your core values, priorities, goals, and activities will maximize personal effectiveness and enhance your ability to achieve lifelong pursuits.

CONCLUSION

Habits are extremely important for success. Researchers have discovered that successful habits are the foundation of success in any career. Whether delivering a presentation in the corporate boardroom, managing a time-sensitive, high-profile project, securing a commitment from a wealthy donor, or preparing for a major sports event, the essential ingredients for outstanding performance can be found in a person's ingrained habits.

World-class habits are not always evident to the average person. Most Americans are rarely introduced to top entrepreneurs. Moreover, even if introduced at a single event, they are unable to benefit from repetitive observations and nuances of the best-in-class habits of America's top professionals. The fastest way to develop the essential skills and habits of wealthy entrepreneurs has been through a mentor. When mentors are not available, the next best approach is to study those who represent—and have demonstrated—the best practices in their fields. In this regard, we have focused our study on the winning habits of Steve Jobs.

Steve Jobs was not born into wealth. *The Winning Habits of Steve Jobs* is a story about one remarkable individual who came from humble beginnings to reach the pinnacle of power in the age of information technologies. While many billionaires may have come from a wealthy background, Steve was a man of his own making. That made him a premier candidate for observation when it comes to the study of winning habits. Steve's mother abandoned him at an early age. His working-class family had none of the trappings of wealth. In many ways, Steve forged these winning habits on his own.

Entrepreneurs such as Steve Jobs are rare. These extremely wealthy people are less than .1 percent of the world's population, yet these entrepreneurs all carry a mark of distinction. They are world-class entrepreneurs within their selected fields of expertise. Through long-term vision, financial acumen, and painstaking attention to detail, they have created a competitive advantage over their competitors. Steve stands out as a rare individual who was not born into a wealthy family and tradition. He developed best-in-class habits and skills through hard work and determination.

Steve Jobs became a household name in America, but it didn't happen overnight. He spent a lifetime developing skills and enduring habits that would improve the way he approached strategic vision, innovation, networking, management, recruitment, focus on customer needs, and learning how to be a CEO. Steve did not begin his career with these habits. With persistence and desire, he instituted many of the remarkable habits that carried him through the difficult years and brought him to the peak of success as an entrepreneur, innovator, and CEO.

You can learn and apply the winning habits of Steve Jobs in your field. Instead of applying a trial-and-error approach to development, apply the habits you've observed in this book as a blueprint for action. Fostering an inquisitive mind, following your passion, visualizing your future, setting short-term and long-term goals, seeking mentors, networking with the right partners, developing an uncommon focus, and innovating by connecting the dots are some of the topics we addressed. By observing the experiences of Steve Jobs, we have gained valuable insights into the relative value of the habits in practice. Apply these winning habits—and you will have started on the path to remarkable success in your field.

ENDNOTES

1. Dr. Stephanie Donaldson-Pressman, Rebecca Jackson, and Dr. Robert Pressman, *The Learning Habit: A Groundbreaking Approach to Parenting that Helps Our Children Succeed in School and Life* (New York: The Penguin Group, 2014).
2. *Merriam-Webster*, s.v. "habit," accessed 2016, *http://www.merriam-webster.com/dictionary/habit*.
3. Ibid.
4. Charles Duhigg, *The Power of Habits: Why We Do What We Do in Life and Business* (New York: Random House Trade Paperback, 2014), 14–18.
5. Kathleen McAuliffe, "If Modern Humans Are So Smart, Why Are Our Brains Shrinking?" *Discover Magazine*, January 20, 2011, *https://www.discovermagazine.com/the-sciences/if-modern-humans-are-so-smart-why-are-our-brains-shrinking*.
6. Thomas C. Corley, *Rich Habits: The Daily Success Habits of Wealthy Individuals* (Minneapolis, MN: Langdon Street Press, 2009), 37–43.
7. Kim Painter, "Want to Adopt a New Habit? 'Stack It,'" *USA Today*, August 25, 2015, 1; S. J. Scott, *Habit Stacking: 97 Small Life Changes That Take Five Minutes*

or Less (Van Nuys, CA: New Castle Publishing Co, 2014), 1.

8. Rebecca Jackson, "Study Finds Habits in Children Take Root by Age 9," *Psychology Today*, February 25, 2015, 1.

9. Tom Corley, *Change Your Habits, Change Your Life: Strategies that Transformed 177 Average People into Self-Made Millionaires* (Minneapolis, MN: North Loop Books, 2016), 12–13.

10. Robert T. Kiyosaki and Sharon L. Lechter, *Rich Dad, Poor Dad* (New York: Warner Books, 2011), 13–17.

11. Jean Rodes, "Top Twenty-Five Mentoring Relationships in History," *The Chronicle of Evidence Based Mentoring*, September 13, 2015, 1; "Three Famous Billionaire Entrepreneurs and their Mentors," *Mentorship BC*, February 12, 2015, 1.

12. "Steve's Two Jobs," *Time*, October 18, 1999, 1–4.

13. Connie Guglielmo, "A Day in the Life of Steve Jobs," *Forbes*, May 7, 2012, 1.

14. John C. Maxwell, "The Daily Routine of Successful Leaders," *Success*, August 15, 2014, 1.

15. August Turak, "Steve Jobs and the One Trait All Innovative Leaders Share," *Forbes*, November 21, 2011, 1.

16. Carolyn Sun, "Four Successful Habits You Can Learn from Jeff Bezos, the World's Third Richest Person," *Entrepreneur*, July 26, 2016, 2.

17. Alp Mimaroglu, "Five Habits that Made Elon Musk an Innovator," *Entrepreneur*, May 3, 2016, 1.

18. Minda Zetlin, "Eight Highly Effective Habits that Helped Make Bill Gates the Richest Man on Earth," *Inc. Magazine*, May 3, 2016, 1.
19. Shana Lebowitz, "Even as a Kid, Bill Gates Demonstrated This Super-Important Habit of Successful People," *Business Insider*, January 7, 2016, 1.
20. Andrew Merle, "It You Want to Be Like Warren Buffett and Bill Gates, Adopt Their Voracious Reading Habits," Quartz, April 23, 2016, 1.
21. Morgan Quinn, "21 Traits of Highly Successful Billionaires," *GO Banking Rates*, August 18, 2016, 4.
22. Brian De Haaf, "Five Habits of Exceptionally Rich Founders," *Entrepreneur*, September 10, 2015, 1.
23. Walter Isaacson, *Steve Jobs: A Biography by Walter Isaacson* (New York, NY: Simon and Schuster, 2011), 211–212; Randall Stross, *Steve Jobs and the NeXT Big Thing* (New York City, NY: Athenium Books, 1993), 72.
24. Isaacson, 211–212.
25. Bill Murphy Jr., "What Makes Bill Gates So Successful? 7 Key Habits, Practices, and Experiences," *Inc. Magazine*, January 13, 2016, 1.
26. Brian DeHaaff, "Five Habits of Exceptionally Rich Founders," *Entrepreneur*, September 10, 2015, 1.
27. "Mark Zuckerberg Biography: Success Story of Facebook Founder and CEO," *Astrum People* (website, 2016), October 25, 2016.
28. Isaacson, 211–212; Brian Heater, "Key Apple Multi-touch Patent Approved," *PC Magazine*, January 27, 2009, 1.

29. Isaacson, 469; Prince McLean, "Inside the Multi-touch FingerWorks Tech in Apple's Tablet," *Apple Insider*, January 23, 2010, 1; Nicholas Carlson, "And Boy We Have Patented It," *Business Insider*, March 2, 2010, 1.

30. Isaacson, 470–471; Luke Dormehl, "How Corning Won Apple Back and Built the Strongest Gorilla Glass Yet," *Cult of Mac*, November 26, 2014, 1–2, *http://www.cultofmac.com/304120/ corning-gorilla-glass-4*; Adam Williams, "Gorilla Glass Maker Unveils Ultra-Thin and Flexible Willow Glass," *New Atlas*, June 5, 2012, 1.

31. Isaacson, 472; Doug Aamoth, "A Story About Steve Jobs, Steel Balls, and Gorilla Glass," *Time*, January 11, 2013, *https://techland.time.com/2013/01/11/a-story-about-steve-jobs-steel-balls-and-gorilla-glass-you-with-the-cracked-phone-read-this*.

32. Isaacson, 472; Doug Aamoth, "A Story About Steve Jobs, Steel Balls, and Gorilla Glass," *Time*, January 11, 2013, *https://techland.time.com/2013/01/11/a-story-about-steve-jobs-steel-balls-and-gorilla-glass-you-with-the-cracked-phone-read-this*.

33. Isaacson, 472.

34. Isaacson, 472; Jake Nielson, "Ten Innovation Lessons from Steve Jobs and Apple: Story of the iPhone," *The Innovative Manager*, May 21, 2014, 1–4.

35. Isaacson, 384–385; John Gruber, "Getting Steve Jobs Wrong," *Daring Fireball*, November 18, 2011, 1.

36. Isaacson, 384; Jake Nielson, 1–4.

37. Isaacson, 385; Doug Aamoth, "Watch Steve Jobs Unveil the iPod 12 Years Ago," *Time*, October 23, 2013, 1.

38. Richard Feloni, "Mark Cuban Shares the Important Lesson He Learned in his Twenties," *Business Insiders*, March 25, 2015, 1.

39. Walter Isaacson, *Steve Jobs* (New York, NY: Simon and Schuster, 2011), 117. Chapter 11 discussed this phenomenon of the reality distortion field.

40. Isaacson, 118.

41. Isaacson, 119.

42. Isaacson, 359.

43. Isaacson, 166–167; Harry McCracken, "Exclusive: Watch Steve Jobs First Demonstration of the Mac for the Public, Unseen since 1984," *Time*, January 25, 2014, 1.

44. Danny Silk provides this quote in Powerful and Free website. See *https://www.pinterest.com/pin/478929741596038664/activity/*.

45. Isaacson, 27.

46. Isaacson, 82–83; Freek Vermeulen, "Steve Jobs: The Man was Fallible," *Forbes*, October 17, 2011, 1.

47. Isaacson, 152–153; Rhiannon Williams, "John Sculley: 'Steve Jobs Was Misrepresented in Popular Culture,'" *Telegraph*, August 30, 2015, 1.

48. Isaacson, 153.

49. Morgan Quinn, 1–3.

50. Walter Isaacson, *Steve Jobs* (New York, NY: Simon and Schuster, 2011), xix.

51. Isaacson, 348–357; "800,000 iMacs Sold in First 139 Days; iMac Continuing to Attract New Users and Wintel Converts," *PR Newswire*, January 5, 1999, 1.

52. Steve Siebold, *How Rich People Think* (Naperville, IL: Simple Truths, 2010), 4–17.

53. Isaacson, 465; Richard MacManus, "Three Key Business Lessons from Steve Jobs: Intuition, Reinvention, Focus," *ReadWrite*, November 6, 2011, 1.

54. Isaacson, 466; Ryan Block, "The Motorola ROKR E1 Apple iTunes Phone," *Engadget*, September 9, 2005, 1.

55. Isaacson, 329; Kaitlyn Russell, "Twenty-Five Steve Jobs Quotes that Will Change the Way You Work—In the Best Possible Way," *Newsweek*, August 6, 2015, 1.

56. Isaacson, 328; Andy Pike, *Origination: The Geographies of Brands and Branding* (West Sussex, UK: John Wiley and Sons, Ltd), 153.

57. Isaacson, 328; Tom Hormby, "Think Different: The Ad Campaign that Restored Apple's Reputation," *Low End Mac*, August 10, 2013, 1.

58. Isaacson, 328; Rob Siltanen, "The Real Story Behind Apple's 'Think Different' Campaign," *Forbes*, December 14, 2011, 1.

59. Isaacson, 330; Tom Hormby, "Think Different: The Ad Campaign that Restored Apple's Reputation," *Low End Mac*, August 10, 2013, 1.

60. Isaacson, 73–75.

61. Isaacson, 76–77; John Markoff, "An Unknown Co-Founder Leaves after 20 Years of Glory and Turmoil," *Business Day*, September 1, 1997, 1–2.

62. Isaacson, 78; Jason Fell, "Apple's Simple Marketing Manifesto," *Entrepreneur*, October 26, 2011, 1.

63. Isaacson, 78; Richard Trenchard, "Five Business Leaders Who Have a Mentor to Thank for Their Success," *Virgin*, July 8, 2016, 1.

64. John Brownlee, "This LSD Love Guru Gave Steve Jobs his 'Reality Distortion Field,'" *Cult of Mac*, October 24, 2011, 1.

65. "Board of Directors," Ivanhoe Mines New Horizons (website), *https://www.ivanhoemines.com/about/board-of-directors*, 1.

66. Adam Lacshinky, "After 17 Years, Bill Campbell Steps Down from Apple's Board," *Fortune*, July 17, 2014, 1.

67. Brent Schlender and Rick Tetzelli, *Becoming Steve Jobs* (London: Sceptre, 2015), 46–47.

68. Isaacson, 74; Jay Yarrow, "Exclusive: Interview with Apple's First CEO Michael Scott," *Business Insider*, May 24, 2011, 1; Jay Yarrow, "The First Ten Apple Employees: Where are They Now?" *Business Insider*, May 24, 2011, 6.

69. Eric Barker, "32 Ways to Quickly and Easily Improve Your Life," *Business Insider Strategy*, July 13, 2012, 1.

70. Isaacson, 530–531; Walter S. Mossberg, "Apple's MobileMe Is Far Too Flawed to Be Reliable," *Wall Street Journal*, July 24, 2008, *https://www.wsj.com/articles/SB121685869764279343*.

71. Isaacson, 531; Walter S. Mossberg, "Apple's MobileMe is Far Too Flawed to be Reliable," *Wall Street Journal*, July 24, 2008, *https://www.wsj.com/articles/SB121685869764279343*.

72. Isaacson, 491; Rene Ritchie, "Why Apple Would Release a 7-Inch iPad," *iMore*, July 3, 2012, 1.

73. Isaacson, 492; "Apple's Secret Weapon," *Fortune*, June 26, 2012, 1; Chris Foresman, "Apple Awarded Patent for Actual Rounded Rectangle," *Ars Technica*, November 7, 2012.

74. Isaacson, 211–212; Tom Hormby, "The NeXT Years: Steve Jobs Before His Triumphant Return to Apple," *LowEndMac*, August 12, 2008, 1; Gerald C. Lubenow, "Jobs Talks About His Rise and Fall," *Newsweek*, September 29, 1985, 1–2.

75. Isaacson, 219–220; Jacob Morse, "NeXT Logo Presentation—Paul Rand," 10, *http://jacobmorse.com/see/Next_Rand.pdf.*

76. Isaacson, 227; Tom Hormby, "The NeXT Years: Steve Jobs Before His Triumphant Return to Apple," *LowEndMac*, August 12, 2008, 1–4.

77. Jay Yarow, "Steve Jobs Initially Hated the Idea of White Apple Products," *Business Insider*, November 30, 2013, 1.

78. Isaacson, 370; Ken Segall, *Think Simple: How Smart Leaders Defeat Complexity* (New York: Penguin Publishing Group, 2016), 107–124.

79. Isaacson, 370; Ken Segall, 107–124.

80. Isaacson, 376; Gary Hoover, *Hoover's Master List of Major US Companies* (Austin, TX: Hoover's Inc., 2005).

81. Isaacson, 376; Maggie Fazeli Fard, "Fun Facts About the World's First Apple Store," *Washington Post*, May 18, 2011, 1; Philip Elmer DeWitt, "10 Apple Store Numbers," *Fortune Magazine*, May 19, 2011, 1; Joe Wilcox, "What was the First Apple Store Like," BetaNews, May 15, 2011, l.

82. Isaacson, 162; Kimberly Potts, "Five Things You Didn't Know About Apple's '1984' Super Bowl Ad," *Yahoo*, January 29, 2015, 1.

83. Isaacson, 162; Tom Hormby, "The Story Behind Apple's 1984 Ad," *LowEndMac*, January 24, 2014, 1; Jacquelyn Smith, "Experts and Viewers Agree: Apple's '1984' Ad Is the Best Super Bowl Ad of All Time," *Forbes*, January 20, 2012, 1.

84. Isaacson, 164–165; Caroline McCarthy, "Remembering the '1984' Super Bowl Mac Ad," *C/NET*, January 23, 2009, 1.

85. Alan Trapulionis, "Steve Jobs's Definition of 'Smart' Will Reprogram Your Idea of Intelligence," *Entrepreneur's Handbook*, September 7, 2020, *https://entrepreneurshandbook.co/steve-jobss-definition-of-smart-will-make-you-rethink-your-actions-6b1d7873fd46*.

86. Ibid.

87. Professor Loizos Heracleous, "Why Steve Jobs was such a Charismatic Leader?" *Warwick Business School News*, November 11, 2015, 1.

88. Loizos Heracleous and Laura Alexa Klaering, "*Charismatic Leadership and Rhetorical Competence: An Analysis of Steve Jobs' Rhetoric*," *Sage Journals* 39, no. 2 (2014): 131–161.

89. Loizos Heracleous, "Why Steve Jobs was such a Charismatic Leader," Medium (website), December 20, 2016, *https://medium.com/@ashley.potter/why-steve-jobs-was-such-a-charismatic-leader-395edeb6881e*.

90. Isaacson, 199–120; Dave Smith, "Steve Jobs' Death Remembered: Five Lessons the Apple Visionary Leaves Behind," *IBTimes*, October 5, 2014, 1; Zach Miners, "Was Steve Jobs a Jerk? Hiring Case Questions His Character," *PC World*, April 18, 2014, 1.

91. Kimberly Marie Celse, "A Critique of the Leadership Style of Steve Jobs," Touro University Worldwide, February 2, 2014, 1.

92. Isaacson, 120; Dave Smith, "Steve Jobs' Death Remembered: Five Lessons the Apple Visionary Leaves Behind," *IBTimes*, October 5, 2014, 1.

93. Richard Feloni, "Mark Cuban Shares Twelve Secrets to Achieving Extraordinary Success," *Business Insider*, March 31, 2015, 1.

94. Isaacson, 114–115; Andy Hertzfeld, *Revolution in the Valley: The Insanely Great Story of How the Mac Was Made* (Boston, MA: O'Reilly Media, 2004), xxi–xxiv.

95. John Greathouse, "Ten Startup Tips from Steve Jobs," *Corporate Culture, Entrepreneur, Iconic Advice*, October 10, 2011, 1.

96. Isaacson, 133–134; Walter Isaacson, "The Real Leadership Lessons of Steve Jobs," *Harvard Business Review*, April 2012, 1.

INDEX

CPSIA information can be obtained
at www.ICGtesting.com
Printed in the USA
LVHW092355190221
679370LV00005B/330

9 781648 953064